Welcome to Kimmensville
Population 17-1/2

Lisa Church

Welcome to Kimmensville – Population 17-1/2

Copyright © 2017 by Lisa Church

Printed in the United States of America

2017

ISBN 978-0-9862835-1-2 eBook

ISBN 978-0-9862835-2-9 paperback

Churchlady Publishing
Mill Valley, CA

"When you stand and share your story in an empowering way,

your story will heal you and your story will heal somebody else."

– Iyanla Vanzant

Table of Contents

The Summer of 1984   1

Kimmensville Club   17

Eden   31

Mother Goose and Her Goslings   43

The Teachers of St. Barb's   61

Misbehavin'   72

Everybody Loves a Parade...and a Few Cheers   85

The Nun and the Frog   93

Children of the Cornfield   101

Lubba Cheekers   111

Work Hard, Play Hard   120

Teen Angst   133

Until We Meet Again   156

Daniel, My Brother   172

Life A.D.   185

Wally World or Bust   192

Mom's Acting Funny   203

Epilogue   210

Acknowledgements   216

Danny's Drawings   218

The Summer of 1984

We lived a bittersweet life in a Midwestern town where some made it out, others stayed, and one left us way too early. Our neighborhood on Kimmens Road shared laughter, love, small dreams, and big dreams and we had each other when tragedy struck. I am writing this book to share the stories of our cast of characters, especially the story of my beautiful brother, Danny.

Let me start with the muggy weekend in the middle of July, while I was hanging out with my best friends cruising around town, my life changed forever, though not for the better. Dawn, Nancy, and I drove my mom's car on Sunday night to the Canal Days festival. My parents and my younger sister, Amy, were visiting a State Highway Patrol colleague of Dad's that recently moved from Massillon to New Philadelphia, Ohio. Danny assumed he would have the house to himself since Sue was going steady with Chris and it was summer break. He didn't expect our older sister to stay home that night.

My plans were threatened the previous morning when Dad noticed the scratches on Mom's car. It must have happened Friday night at the party downtown. It was clearly a key job from a mean-spirited person. I didn't know my current enemies were going to the same party. Well, maybe I had a feeling they would be there, but I didn't think they would do something so destructive. Of course, we were fighting over a boy.

I should have expected some backlash; the Massillon High girls were always up for a fight. There were scuffles at our school, and we were strong willed people, but it was nothing like the Massillon brawls. Their fights were rumored to involve knives, nunchucks, and a few black kids, all out of the norm at Tuslaw. From my personal experience, you could now add keys to their arsenal.

1

Dad noticed the scratches when he snuck outside for his morning cigarette. We weren't supposed to know he smoked, but we all knew. He stormed in the kitchen door and didn't even bother making a pit stop in the bathroom to wash his hands and rinse his mouth with Listerine. "You were responsible for the car last night, *you* let this happen," Dad yelled as he entered the kitchen from the garage. Holding the door open, he pointed out the gouges in the paint.

Sue, Danny, and I were all eating cereal at the dining room table. Mom was in her bedroom while Amy watched cartoons in the living room. "I don't know what happened!" I screamed back, leaping to my feet. After a few curse words and a reminder of the financial implications of repairing the damage, he ended with, "*You're grounded for the summer!*" and stormed out of the house.

Our school break had just begun, I was sixteen years old with a new driver's license, so I wasn't giving up easily. "*Nooooooo!!*" I shrieked at the thought of being stuck in our brown, brick, ranch-style house wedged between Mrs. Shilling's hog corn field and our family's golf course. I'll be socially ruined by the time my junior year begins, I thought, feeling sorry for myself. "But the festival ends Sunday night, I was supposed to drive. *Please…*" I begged and pleaded as the screen door slammed behind him.

We all knew it was not wise to push him too hard. You don't survive a career with the State Highway Patrol, advancing to sergeant and still have a tranquil nature. When Dad lost his temper, you didn't want to be around. He didn't strike us, except that one time he smacked Sue across the face when she told him to "*Fuck off,*" but he always had the power to hurt us with his words.

There was no sense in arguing, his mind was made up. He backed the car out of the garage and ordered me to hand wash and dry it. I filled an old bucket with cold water from the hose and squirted dishwashing liquid alongside the stream of water until the bubbles were flowing over the sides. I used a sponge to scrub the scrapes, trying to remove the gashes. "*Bitches*," I mumbled to myself, "I'll get them back for ruining my summer and my mom's ride."

It wasn't in the best of shape, but it's all she had, she never complained about Frankie unless he broke down. Mom always named her cars, Frankie Avalon was lucky enough to be the namesake of her brown Ford Fairmont, a sedan that carried just about every kid in our township at some point.

After I had washed the car, Mom drove Danny, Amy, and our neighbor Jimmy to Geauga Lake Amusement Park that Saturday morning to enjoy the beginning of summer. I wasn't able to join them as part of my punishment. I would learn later that I missed out on the filming of my siblings and Jimmy splashing around in a wave pool, which aired that night on the evening news.

Dad and Sue both went to their respective jobs that day. I was happy to have a quiet house so I could sulk and figure out how to get myself out of this situation. I eventually decided to write a letter to a friend I met at camp and put more effort into the oil painting I had started. I wasn't painting as much as I had been a few years ago, but it still relaxed me.

The next morning, I attended Sunday Mass with Mom and Danny. It was always just Mom and the kids, never an explanation as to why Dad was absent. Attending church before school was mandatory, which meant we sat through one-hour ceremonies six days a week for eight years. It was too much. We were burned out and bored. But we dutifully attended so we wouldn't let Mom down. None of us wanted to let Mom down.

On the way to church that morning, I could not stop complaining about Dad grounding me for the summer. I begged Mom to *please* talk to him and explain his judgment was too harsh since it wasn't my fault. "Please, Mom," I begged.

3

After finding a half empty pew towards the back, we performed the obligatory genuflection, the sign of the cross, and then sat quietly. The priest dictated the choreographed movements of standing, sitting, and kneeling. I barely listened to the sermon, mumbling the songs and verses. Danny and I passed notes using the tiny little pencils and the back of the donation envelopes like we did every Sunday.

Sue would normally be sitting next to us, scrawling secret messages and giggling about something funny that one of us noticed. Since she turned eighteen, Sue was able to make the mature decision to abstain from Sunday Mass. My own lack of faith assured that I would ultimately leave the Catholic Church when I reached the legal age, as well. Sue was the first sibling to withdraw. Eventually, we all became recovering Catholics.

I wasn't feeling social. After the final hymn, I dug out the keys from the bottom of Mom's purse so Danny and I could wait in the car, knowing that she would join us after talking to every acquaintance she passed, as well as the priest. We knew from experience we had at least thirty minutes to listen to the radio and stretch out on the car seats while we took in the warmth of the summer sun beaming through the windows.

As we daydreamed in the car, listening to our favorite radio station, WMMS 101.7 FM, I wondered if Danny remembered the last time he was in trouble with Dad like I was right now. I recalled how I had intervened to cover for Danny a couple of months earlier.

I pretended to be his eighteen-year-old sister so the Gold Circle security guards in Canton would release him to me after he was caught shoplifting. He attempted to conceal cassette tapes and men's bikini briefs in his baggy pants, then exited the store without paying.

I pulled off my role with a dress, makeup, heels, and an attitude. After I had signed a legal form swearing I was an adult, Danny was released to my care. We filled Mom in when she

4

returned home from her part-time job at a nursing home. She tried to cover for her precious son, but her attempt was futile.

Dad eventually found out and attended the juvenile court hearing. Knowing I would not be allowed in the courtroom, I rode along to support my brother and read teen magazines in the car. When Danny jumped in the backseat next to me, I sensed a verdict had been handed down.

Forty hours of community service that he would eventually achieve by mowing lawns at the Elms Golf Course for Aunt Margaret, as well as a ban from all Gold Circle stores. No one mentioned to Dad that Margaret slipped Danny ten dollars each week for his "community service."

My dad was upset and humiliated. After a career of catching and punishing lawbreakers, his child dared to cross that line. *"You are an embarrassment! I am ashamed to call you my son!"* Dad yelled angrily at Danny's reflection in the rear-view mirror as we left the courthouse.

He later apologized for his outburst, but at the time Danny's shoulders sunk and his head dropped to his chest. He seemed to get what a total disappointment he was to our dad that day. I also saw anger in both of their eyes.

Mom's knock on the window shook us back into reality. We left the church parking lot heading to the Elms Country Club for my summer job at the swimming pool snack bar. My begging and pleading continued only because my mother was a very patient woman who usually sided with her kids, so I knew I could eventually wear her down. "I'm a good student, play sports, work, *and* babysit. This *one* mistake should not warrant being stuck at home for the *entire* summer. *Pleeeaassssee…will you talk to Dad*?!"

Danny was silent during my unrelenting tantrum. He was sitting in the back of the Ford, straddling the middle seat and looking very intense, wringing his hands, and furrowing his brow.

Danny's relationship with our dad waned as my brother grew into an incredibly compassionate, artistic, and thoughtful young man. Dad thought his only son would enjoy the hobbies he lived for--hunting, fishing, and camping--but they just weren't Danny's idea of a good time. He would never shoot an animal, under any circumstances, Dad could never understand this conviction when he considered it a sport and a means to feed his family.

Danny also didn't approve of the way Dad talked to the girls in the family at times. We were Danny's girls, all four of us. Dan the Man, as we affectionately called him, was very protective of his brood.

As we drove down the bumpy Elms driveway past rolling green hills with picnic tables next to tennis courts, I didn't realize it at the time, but I think Danny was weighing his options. I whipped my head around to say goodbye and saw a set of dark, cold eyes returning my gaze. I knew my brother and his moods well. I knew that my situation, as well as my reaction, had bothered him immensely. He must have felt helpless.

He looked down at his hands as I was getting out of the car. Mom assured me that we would talk when I got home. I dried my tears and walked up the sidewalk towards the pool. Danny didn't jump out and get in the front seat like he normally would. He stayed in the back, alone, deep in thought as Mom drove up the lane.

My shift at the snack bar dragged on all afternoon. I sold popcorn and candy bars to dripping wet kids. In between customers, I stewed about my situation and wondered if my mom was actually protesting the reprimand on my behalf.

When Aunt Margaret returned from her errands, she released me from my duties. I was grateful for the time it would

6

take to walk past the driving range and along the tree line of the golf course to our house half a mile away. I didn't want to cross paths with my father and hoped he was in his den in the basement, where he spent so much of his time alone at home.

He had no idea that Danny and Jimmy had infiltrated his private lair by taking the hinges off the padlocked door one weekend when he was away at a shooting match. They also stole some of his porn magazines, which they, in turn, stashed at the barn for future visits.

After my leisurely walk, I noticed the truck was not in the driveway but the damaged Fairmont was still sparkling in the sun from my washing. I found my mom in her bedroom folding laundry. I bounced on the bed, stretched out on my dad's side, and crossed my arms behind my head. After a bit of idle chit chat about my day at the Elms, I was trying not to sound too anxious when I asked her if she had talked to Dad about reconsidering my sentence.

Mom didn't like confrontation, especially with her husband, so I was not surprised she hadn't spoken to him. I also knew she didn't like to disappoint her children and probably had devised another scheme. She wouldn't let me down.

That evening, it was very unlike my mother to hurry Amy and Dad out the door to make sure they weren't late for dinner at their friend's house. There could be traffic on the Interstate, she said. Mom was inherently late for everything in life. It wasn't out of the ordinary for us to wait over an hour to be picked up after school.

Being locked out at home and stuck sitting on the rusty freezer in the garage was a regular occurrence as we waited for Mom to pull into the driveway. She always had excuses and the names of the people she ran into with stories about how she just couldn't get away. It was frustrating, but we were used to it, and we knew if we were the person in need, Mom would be there for us. That evening, I knew bustling everyone out of the house was part of her plot. She snuck me the car keys when Dad wasn't looking.

As the red taillights from my dad's truck disappeared, I hastily threw on the clothes I had secretly planned to wear earlier that day. I slapped on some makeup, ran my fingers through my messy curls, and brushed my teeth in preparation for my escape. I promised Mom I'd be home before them, so Dad would never know I took the car and went out against his wishes. I did wonder briefly, as I checked the contents of my purse if he wrote down the mileage. I knew Dad didn't trust his teenagers or my mom so I wouldn't put it past him. If he did, I'd deal with that later.

Danny was lying on the couch watching TV when I headed to the garage. I hadn't talked to him much after work. He was very reserved all afternoon and spent most of his time pencil-sketching a boy crouched down against a wall with his arms around his knees, only the top of his head and eyes peeking out, a tear running down his cheek. I had glanced over Danny's shoulder and complimented his drawing. He mumbled his appreciation but never looked up.

I told him I was leaving for the night and elaborated on the story I worked out with Mom. He agreed to cover for my deception if Dad called or returned early, adding that he could improve on my outfit that evening by lending me his clothes. Danny was quite the stylist.

My brother led me to his room and opened his closet door to pull out a new shirt that I knew was one of his favorites. Mom let us shop for school clothes during summer break, as long as we promised not to wear them until school started. Yeah, right. Danny convinced me that the white polo shirt he was recommending would be flattering with the shorts I was wearing.

He was dressed in a white, sleeveless T-shirt with a graffiti print on the front and a pair of black sports shorts. I had mentioned that I liked the shirt he was wearing and would

8

appreciate it if he let me borrow it sometimes, as well. He smiled and promised that I could. I thanked my brother as I grabbed my purse and headed to the garage, reminding him that Dad could not find out I had taken the car. He agreed to keep my secret, following me down the hallway where I thought he would stop in the kitchen and get a snack. He made a dessert that morning that we all found irresistible.

Danny's famous brownies had peanut butter weaved into the gooey chocolate fudge and crumbled peanuts sprinkled on top. He made them from a box mix, but they always turned out perfectly when he baked them. The brownies would be the first thing I'd see on the counter when I returned from the hospital.

I jumped in the brown Ford Fairmont and was backing into the street when I noticed Danny walking down the driveway. I stopped the car and started to roll down the window, he just waved and smiled. I waved back and yelled, "Bye!" As I slowly drove down Kimmens Road, dodging pot holes, I looked in the rearview mirror of the car and saw my brother standing in the street, looking in my direction. I adjusted the mirror and stared back, wondering why he was making such a big deal of my leaving. I assumed he was worried that I would get caught by Dad and was concerned for my well-being.

Dawn wasn't ready when I arrived to pick her up, of course. She was never punctual. I managed to find a best friend that rivaled my mother when it came to tardiness. And like Mom, Dawn enjoyed life and didn't let something silly like a schedule get in her way. To be a friend of Dawn's meant accepting her free spirit and not stressing out if you showed up and she had rollers in her hair. I hung out and talked to her mom, Ruthie, while she primped for our evening. When Dawn was finally ready to face the public, we headed north on Kenyon to Butterbridge Road and up the long driveway to Nancy's beautiful, sprawling home. She was waiting for us outside, boom box in hand, excited about our adventure.

Nancy jumped in the brown Ford, and our trio was complete. My parents wouldn't spring for a cassette player in the old beater, so we were left with the abysmal AM/FM radio choices. This is why we always brought a boom box with a variety of cassette tapes when we took Frankie. Nancy popped in Meat Loaf's *Bat out of Hell*--and that's precisely the way I drove toward downtown Canal Fulton for the festival we had all been anticipating.

A suggestion was made that we stop along the way at a convenience store and use Nancy's fake ID to pick up some Schaefer beer to get our night started. It was less than three dollars for a six-pack, including tax, which is probably why the advertising slogan was "Schaefer is the one beer to have when you're having more than one." It's the only beer high school kids could afford when they were looking for a little buzz.

The ID worked like a charm, even though it should not have. Nancy did not resemble a twenty-four-year-old but was still allowed to purchase beer and cigarettes. She always made a grand effort to apply a bit of extra makeup and hairspray on the evenings we'd be putting her sister's driver's license to the test. It was also the confidence that Nancy exuded when she walked into the store and headed directly for the beer aisle as if she did this on her way home from work every night.

My girlfriends and I sipped the weak, lukewarm beer and gossiped about the boys we hoped would be at the festival and those we would rather avoid. I steered the car along the winding, narrow streets as we rocked out to '80s music. We eventually arrived at Heritage Park near the studio where my cousin Colleen and I took painting lessons from Mrs. Stiles each Saturday. Those weekends always brought back good memories, but I was distracted by the lack of sights and sounds that we would usually see at Canal Days.

Where was the Ferris wheel they always parked next to the canal? The block should have been alive with the lights and sounds of the celebration, children circling the fairgrounds as they devoured candied apples. I expected parked cars would occupy every free spot within blocks. The three of us sat in confused silence for a few moments when we realized the fair was not happening. "I guess it was only Friday and Saturday," Dawn finally said, stating the obvious.

We decided to cruise around Massillon, find something to do. I cracked open my second lager and took a sip before I turned Frankie around and headed back to where we started. Pat Benatar was our choice of tunes on the drive back to Massillon. We sang the lyrics with the attitude this song deserved as we shook our hair-sprayed manes, "Well you're the *real* tough cookie with the long history, of breaking little hearts, like the one in me..." When we reached the chorus, we pumped our fists in the air and belted out in unison, "*Hit me with your best shot...Fire away...*" It was a very empowering song, giving us a rush to sing along with such a badass female musician.

After everything I did to manipulate my way out of the house the second night of my summer-long punishment, I had no regrets. My two allies and I drove through the Burger Town parking lot looking for familiar cars and faces. If it were a Friday night after a football game, and not a random Sunday in the middle of summer, the fast food joint would be packed with high school kids overflowing from the restaurant to the parking lot. That was not the scene on this particular evening. We parked the old Ford and used the facilities.

The watery beer we drank required us to pee frequently, and I wasn't sure of our next opportunity with actual amenities since our plans were to cruise through the hangouts closer to home. The restrooms in our school district usually consisted of a cornfield on Beaumont Drive or a ditch on some dark road using whatever scraps of tissue or scratchy, fast food napkin we could unearth from the glove box. After checking our reflections in the mirror and reapplying our lip gloss, we disappointedly walked back outside. "Where is everyone tonight? *Damn*, it's summer break," we complained.

11

We drove the streets of Meadowlake Estates hoping to find a few kids from school. It was eerily empty that evening, and the lake was still. We grabbed the last six-pack, parked ourselves on a picnic table to finish another brew, and enjoy another smoke. We usually shared a pack on the weekends, and then one of us would be assigned the duty of concealing the remaining cigarettes until our next adventure. This time it was my turn. I never looked forward to this responsibility, but I was relieved later that evening when I needed them to calm my nerves.

Our excursion was turning out to be a disappointment, and we were getting hungry. Or maybe we were just bored and decided to eat because we weren't sure what else to do until our 11 p.m. curfews. I pointed the Fairmont south, and we drove, once again, towards downtown, passing an uncommonly deserted Lawson's parking lot.

Wendy's was never considered a popular hangout for teenagers in Massillon, but we gave up on the possibility of seeing other friends or running into one of our crushes. At this point, we just wanted some greasy fries and hamburgers to soak up the beer, so we ended up at Wendy's solely because of the proximity.

Dawn, Nancy, and I ordered our unwholesome meals and carried our trays through the empty restaurant. We settled at a table near the parking lot with views of Lincoln Way through the terrarium-style windows they were known for in the 1980s. We wolfed down our burgers. It was only eight thirty, and we could think of nothing else to do.

I slowed down and savored my deep-fried potatoes and Coke when I swore I heard a siren. I recalled the nightmare I had a few months earlier. What did it mean? Why would an ambulance with sirens and lights blaring pull into the driveway of Wendy's while it was packed full of customers?

In my dream, Dawn, Nancy, and I were some of those patrons. We were also sitting close to the window that evening nearest the driveway and were shocked when the ambulance stopped right outside our window. The driver turned off the siren but left the spinning lights on before he exited and casually walked to the back of the bus. The paramedic opened the double doors and slowly pulled out the gurney supporting its victim, looking me directly in the face with a sad but questioning expression. The injured passenger was Danny.

I hazily realized the EMT was asking me to identify my lifeless brother through the window of Wendy's. He looked as if he were sleeping. I stood up and began screaming at the sight, which is when I awoke from this terrifying vision. I sat upright in the dark and realized, once I got my bearings, that I was safe at home, which meant the same for Danny. I had sighed with relief, wiping away the tears and sweat, grateful it was only a nightmare.

I thought Dawn would have some insight into why I had had such a creepy and unsettling image of my brother. Dawn was a perceptive soul and had declared with conviction to a few close friends that she had brushes with the afterlife. We believed her. I had asked Dawn her opinion of this dream. She wouldn't say, but she secretly hoped it wasn't a premonition of some sort.

I didn't want to think about something so depressing and bring everyone down, so I didn't mention the dream in front of Nancy or remind Dawn. I asked if they heard a siren, they didn't.

We finished our food and headed out to the parking lot. Nancy and Dawn took turns sitting in the front seat each time we stopped. No one liked to ride in the backseat alone, plus in this car that meant you were the DJ.

I wheeled the car eastbound since we agreed to make one more jaunt through town before professing defeat. We all enjoyed our last beers and another cigarette with the windows down, listening to a cassette tape that Dawn mixed as we motored through Massillon for the last time that evening. After finding absolutely nothing exciting to do or anyone home to visit, we finally agreed to head down Orrville Street and drop Nancy off first.

As we turned right onto Butterbridge, we all chewed a piece of gum and sprayed perfume in an attempt to mask the smell of beer and smoke. I turned left into her driveway and ascended up the long lane with the headlights still on high beam from the dark roads in our neighborhoods. Her parents slept on the other side of the estate, so I didn't think my lights would disturb them.

I was shocked to see Nancy's mother standing outside in her robe, slippers, and hair curlers. Her hands were gripping the top of her gown. She looked terrified. Irene ran to the open car window and yelled for us to go to Dawn's house quickly. "Your mom called, you *must* go home now, Dawn!" Nancy got out of the car, her mother put her arm around her and led her to the back door. She whispered something into her daughter's ear, Nancy put her hands over her face and sobbed, her shoulders crumbling. Irene grabbed Nancy and hugged her tightly. They looked back at us in the high beams. Pure heartache in their eyes.

I screeched back down the driveway and sped toward Dawn's house. What was happening? Someone was hurt. Who? My friend lived a mile and a half from Nancy with only one stop sign between them, we would know the truth soon. I made the typical three-minute drive in two. Dawn was afraid something happened to her dad or brother, Kenny. I tried my best to reassure her.

Shortly after ten o'clock, we approached the lush trees and plants that draped both sides of Dawn's driveway. I was stunned to see the car belonging to Chris, my sister Sue's boyfriend, alongside another distressed figure donned in a robe. It was Dawn's mom. Ruthie had her arm around my sister. This was too much. How long had they been there and what in the hell was going on?

14

My mind raced wildly as I skid the car to a halt, now assuming the bad news was about my parents and Amy. Were they in a car accident tonight while on their way home from the Merriman's house? Something had happened to my six-year-old sister, I feared. Dawn jumped from the car first and ran to her worried mother who embraced her as she demanded answers. I ran frantically towards Sue and Chris and shouted, "What's *wrong*? What's *happened*?"

Everything seemed too slow, as in a bad dream. Instead of answering me, my eldest sibling grabbed my arm with the most painful expression I had ever seen on her face as she shakily said, "Get in the car *now*, Lisa," and firmly pushed me into the backseat behind Chris. I was numb but knew I needed to listen to her, something serious was happening.

As Chris sped out the driveway, I could hear Dawn. She was screeching like an animal. Sue turned to me crying, took my hand and said, "Danny shot himself, Lisa." My body stiffened. Then I started trembling. I managed to ask her, "Where? Where did he get shot? What do you mean?" My first thought was he was playing with one of Dad's guns from the rack in the living room and hit his toe or something. Firearms were accessible to us. The entire family knew the key was under the wooden mallard duck on top on the gun rack. It had to be an accident.

Sue looked me in the eyes again, her face wet, "In the head. He shot himself in the head." A piercing shriek exited my lungs as I tried to acknowledge the words I just heard from my sister. I would learn later from Dawn that she heard my horrific screams as we drove down Kenyon.

I frantically shook my head back and forth. *I just saw him.* I tried to convince myself, *he can't die, he's fourteen. I can't lose my only brother. "Faster!! Drive faster, Chris! I have to see him now!"* I bawled as I grabbed Chris' shoulders from the backseat and shook him. He was already speeding to the hospital, he couldn't go fast enough. I wanted to reverse time and live this evening all over again. I couldn't wrap my head around what I had just heard. The hospital was less than a ten-minute drive from Dawn's house. It felt like an eternity.

Chris pulled into the ER entrance, tires squealing, I leaped from the car before he came to a complete stop. I ran through the automatic doors and screamed at the nurses, *"Where is he? I have to see my brother! Where is Danny?!!"* A nurse jumped up to assist me and calm me down as I heard my name being cried out.

I looked down the corridor. My parents were running toward me weeping, my mother with her arms outstretched, utter misery and panic seizing her face. They pulled me into them and sobbed uncontrollably. That's when I knew in my heart, I would never see my little brother alive again.

Kimmensville Club

Kimmensville had a population of seventeen and a half when the street signs were installed by our "Mayor" Ronnie Lowers. The half was referring to my cousin Andy who was still in Aunt Leanne's womb when the adults decided to christen the neighborhood. Naming our close-knit quarter after our street, Kimmens Road, was Ronnie's idea during one of the many afternoon barbecues hosted at the Lowers residence during the humid, summer months. Too bad the sign maker misspelled it as Kimm*i*nsville. We were an easy-going bunch, so didn't bother having it corrected. We knew who we were.

The five plots of land that were gifted to my mom and her four siblings by their father after they were all married stretched a tenth of a mile down Kimmens and lined the back nine of the Elms Golf Course. Howard Black found it to be the quietest spot on the twenty-seven-hole golf course he created. My grandfather hoped his kids would raise their families together on the land where he worked so hard to build his dream.

Howard's three youngest children fulfilled that dream and eventually built their homes in a row in the order in which they were born. The open space and warm summers in Northeast Ohio allowed us all to plant gardens; two families had barns that housed horses and ponies. We all had dogs that were mostly named after presidents, and some homes had swimming pools, basketball hoops, or trampolines.

I loved taking in the fresh morning air from our back deck while relishing in the silence before tee time, enjoying the undisturbed dew drops perched on the tip of random blades of grass. The fog often hovered over the course and created an eerie effect that was mesmerizing. I think these experiences are why I started waking up before my family and drinking Folgers instant coffee at twelve years old.

Aunt Nancy was living in Florida with her strapping, ex-NFL husband and opted out of the quaint life in the rural city of Massillon for warmer weather and more exotic surroundings. When his three siblings broke ground on their first homes, Uncle Bob was raising his two boys in California with his wife, Marla.

One of the relinquished lots accommodated a yellow, split-level house on the edge of the twenty-first green that was sold to Ronnie and his wife, Doris Lowers, and where they raised their three children.

The second parcel was the earliest dwelling on the street. A beautiful, white farmhouse sat adjacent to the Lowers and was built in the mid-1800s when the land was a cattle farm instead of a golf course. We lived in the farmhouse for a few years after Dad's Army tour in Germany ended and before we built our home two lots east on Kimmens Road.

I cherished the time we inhabited the old, two-story home with the looming buckeye tree at the end of the driveway. The front porch, pleasantly shaded by elm trees, overlooked the cornfield across the street. I loved our Pepto-Bismol pink bedroom walls and frilly white curtains that made Sue and me feel like princesses. Though, I did find the home immense and creepy at times with the damp cement basement, spooky attic above the garage, and the squawking bats that swished through the darkness and sprawled their wings across the tree trunks when they wanted to rest.

When Sue was four, and I was three, we decided to spruce up the house with our crayons and drew the toddler rendition of *Starry Night* on the outside of the house, so it was viewable by anyone approaching from the driveway. My father wasn't as pleased as we expected him to be since he always enjoyed our artistic creations in the past. This marked our first disobedient episode on Kimmens Road where the kids would reign for the next thirteen years.

Our original headquarters was the brick smokehouse next to the old, red barn that separated the farmhouse from the apple orchard and golf course. The livestock was long gone and the barn now housed rusted tractors and broken golf carts. The children were forbidden to enter it alone by every parent on the street, which just made it even more enticing.

There was quite a bit of trouble to be had in that barn before the parents petitioned my mom's cousin, who was managing the course by then, to have it and the meat house demolished. The danger of missing floorboards tempting a pitfall to the ground below and our fascination with consuming and bathing in the tractor oils and degreasers assured our parents they were making the right decision.

We had pulled off plenty of mischievous deeds before the momentous day all of the kids surrounded the old structures and watched in awe as a bulldozer destroyed some of the fondest memories of our childhood. I wondered if Danny and Jimmy thought to grab their stash of porn magazines hidden on the bottom floor of the barn that they slowly collected from each of their father's secret hoard. Something told me they had remembered.

When we discovered the small brick house that sat next to the barn, we pried open the wooden door and noticed the chipped plaster walls and two small windows. Rusted meat hooks were protruding from the wooden beams on the ceiling. I froze in the doorway, imagining the sights and smells of death that floated from this little hut when it was used for its original purpose of preserving raw beef. All of the neighborhood kids agreed, with a little care and attention it had potential.

We asked my parents if we could use the building as a clubhouse. We pleaded that we didn't need much help from the adults for this renovation. If we could have some supplies and paint, we would spend the afternoon fixing it up to our liking. My father agreed to remove the meat hooks and provide paint and brushes to keep us occupied with a project, and hopefully prevent us from causing trouble.

Technically, the barn and brick house belonged to Aunt Margaret and her family since they bought the golf course from Grandpa. We took the liberty on more than this occasion, based on the fact that we were family and the building had not been used for thirty years.

Sandy donated old kitchen curtains that she begged from Doris to cover the tiny windows. Sandy Lowers was the oldest of the posse that ran free creating adventures and havoc in the neighborhood. She was a beautiful, petite, popular blonde and the envy of all the girls in the neighborhood. Doris was a secretary at a law firm, and Ronnie owned a used car lot and a tow truck business. On her sweet sixteenth, the baby of the family was handed the keys to a baby blue Cutlass Supreme with a white top and matching leather seats. The stereo was fully loaded with an eight-track player. My brother had a crush on Sandy until she started getting boyfriends of her own and he realized with the four-year age difference, he could never compete, so just admired her from afar.

Karlene, who was next in age rank to Sandy, ran home and snuck a rug from her parents while they were at work, which added to the ambiance of the cabin. Karlene and her family bought Aunt Judi's house when she moved to Florida with Uncle John and their daughter, Dena. Karlene had an older stepsister, Jenny, that came around every other weekend, but she didn't pay much attention to us. The first thing their mom did was remove the vintage wallpaper covered with naked women from the bathroom wall. The taste between Judi and Bev was like comparing hippy chic to old country charm, so the redecorating began immediately.

Bev was the most stylish mom on the block and took pleasure in hosting home interior parties for her girlfriends. Karlene was the cynic of our group but also the first to break into laughter when we were joking around or performing for the parents in some creative fashion. Karlene's unique laugh was contagious enough to make the rest of us join along. She sounded like a young whooping crane, only more musical. Karlene was also the first of the girls to develop a real chest and wasn't quite sure what to do with the attention it brought from the boys, while the rest of us were stuffing our training bras with toilet paper.

Sue and I covered the interior of our new clubhouse with a glossy, light yellow coat of paint that was left over from a kitchen project, while the other kids gathered supplies from their various houses.

Jimmy Espinosa lived in the farmhouse now and had the closest walk to scour for goods. He and Danny returned with an old table and a stool that they found in his dad's workshop in their two-car garage. Mr. Espinosa often wore a groovy *Keep on Truckin'* T-shirt, which all the kids coveted, and was a member of the Van Club. We thought he was pretty cool and hoped he wouldn't find out we had borrowed some things without his permission.

My cousin Colleen returned carrying her stash for the clubhouse along with a big grin, brown curls bouncing around her adorable, round, freckled face. This assignment was right up Aunt Leanne's alley, the quintessential homemaker. Colleen was hauling old pillows for us to sit on and a glass jar under her arm to ultimately display the wildflowers we would pick from the perimeter of the barn, along with a bag of banana chips Leanne bought on her last jaunt to Amish country.

After we had moved out, Uncle Jim's family lived in the farmhouse as a staging ground while their new home was being constructed next door. Colleen was the eldest, followed by Tommy and Andy, with Joe being welcomed into the family only months before they would leave Kimmensville. Their house was smack dab between our new home and the farmhouse.

21

As we decorated, we all imagined it would be so much fun to have our own little meeting place, and that is exactly what transpired. Our clubhouse was physically complete, but our clique was still lacking an identity. While the second coat of paint was drying, we roamed the golf course and climbed apple trees in the orchard.

Later that afternoon, our first meeting at the clubhouse was called to order, we decided the first piece of business was to determine the name of our congregation. We ate the banana chips along with Little Debbie snack cakes confiscated from my household for our opening ceremony and brainstormed names to identify our circle of friends. After laughing over some of the juvenile and foul suggestions contributed mostly by the boys, we unanimously voted on Kimmensville Club in honor of the community our parents inaugurated and the close union our gang had formed at such a young age.

The day Jimmy and his family had moved into the farmhouse, my siblings and I saw him playing with his Tonka truck in the driveway. We wandered over to meet the new neighbors and hoped the youngest of their three kids would be someone worthy of our time. Danny was looking forward to hanging out with a boy his age since he was outnumbered by the girls at home and on Kimmens.

Jimmy's parents would soon realize they had to keep an eye on us when we all hung out together. They didn't hear us convince their son that we should unpack the gigantic, red, faux leather bean bag we eyed in the U-Haul and place it directly below the attic landing, which happened to be two floors above the lush, green grass in their backyard.

Sandy and Karlene joined us as we climbed the steep, wooden staircase that ran diagonally up the back of the house leading to the attic above the garage. Facing the backyard, my daredevil brother grabbed the railing and swung his legs out to gain speed while aiming for the bean bag. He released his grasp and landed squarely on the sack. Mid-air, Jimmy crossed his legs in a sitting position, also nailing the target while his new friends cheered. Sandy was next, followed by me, Karlene, and then Sue.

The impact of each jump stretched the seams of the bean bag until they could no longer contain the twelve cubic feet of tiny, white, polystyrene balls. When I hurled my chubby self from the landing for the second time, the beads sprayed from the holes like fire hoses and softly floated to the ground where they embedded themselves in the blades of grass.

Mr. and Mrs. Espinosa ran towards the loud explosion the bag made on impact, noticing their backyard now resembled a frost in July. Except this winter wonderland did not melt, and each time he mowed his lawn that summer, Mr. Espinosa was reminded of his charming, new neighbors. We knew immediately that Jimmy was going to acclimate just fine, and Danny had a new best friend.

One day during a clubhouse gathering, someone noticed a field mouse scurrying along the floor. After we had finished shrieking and leaping around the small room, we trapped it under a five-gallon plastic bucket that was flipped upside down and used as an extra stool. Sue scooted a piece of wood under the bucket to cover the opening as we turned it right side up, entrapping the little, gray rodent. The hay Danny and Jimmy found in the barn was placed on the bottom of the pail and intended to keep him warm, but it may have ended up providing leverage for the big escape.

KC was an obvious name for our new mascot since it was the acronym of our new society. Not to mention every red-blooded teen raised in the U.S. in the mid-1970s enjoyed jiggling to the hit, *Shake Your Booty* by the funk group KC and the Sunshine Band. We discussed how we planned to keep our new pet in the clubhouse and take turns feeding him before someone came up with the brilliant idea that we should introduce the little critter to my mom.

23

The group of kids found my mother in her bedroom folding clothes. We burst into the room with the bucket flopping side to side and KC getting thrown around like a sock in a dryer. We realized instantly that Mom was not pleased with our decision to bring the mouse into her private space, we still begged her to look at his adorable face and his cute, little nose when he twitched his whiskers. We chased Mom around the room laughing at her squeamishness and didn't see KC flee. Danny pushed the dry straw around to be sure our little friend wasn't hiding.

Regrettably for us, he had escaped. Mom refused to stay in her own room so she squeezed into one of our twin beds every night for a week before she could sleep soundly in the sanctuary of her own boudoir again.

The denizens of Kimmens Road not only nicknamed their neighborhood, and elected Ronnie as the Mayor, but they assigned each other roles in our community. After a few beers at a Lower's barbecue when the kids were outside of earshot, they gave each other silly titles based on their personalities or professions.

Ronnie's wife, the hostess, was affectionately nominated as the Town Slut. I didn't ask. My parents were quickly identified as the Sherriff and Mother Goose since my dad had spent his career at the Ohio State Highway Patrol and Mom was never without a circle of children around her ankles. My mother attracted children like the pied piper fascinated them with his magic pipe. Her antithesis was her brother Jim who changed religions as often as he changed his socks, Mormon this time, so he was appropriately designated as the Preacher. Judi's husband, John, liked to consume a few beers after finishing his US Postal route, so John earned the original title of Town Drunk. After Judi and John had moved, Karlene's stepfather, Gene, not only occupied their home, he inherited the same honor. Gene had a heart of gold and was known to nap on the couch in their family

24

room most afternoons after a few beers and a slurred announcement.

It was also during one of these boisterous get-togethers when my mom revealed her exciting but shocking news. The sun was setting over the golf course, the coals on the grill cooled off, and the mosquitoes were quietly buzzing. The kids were inside watching television sprawled out on the red, shag carpet, soaking in the air conditioning.

My parents expected the three children they were raising would complete their family, little did they know we would not be whole until our baby sister arrived. Mom shared that eight years after her last born, her three kids would be gaining a new sibling. The neighborhood was ecstatic with the idea of having another little one running wild through Kimmensville and creating memories and adventures of their own. Karlene's mom asked my parents if they had picked out any names for their new addition. My dad, with his typical sarcastic wit, replied that he was trying to decide between, "The End" and "Boo Boo."

Amy's birth was the end of the childbearing years for my mother, but it signified a new beginning for our family. Amy brought so much joy and laughter to our lives. We lovingly nicknamed her Boo Boo because she was an unexpected surprise to our family.

I'm sure they reconsidered their fourth child hours after Amy was born, not because of a difficult birth or an unruly newborn. They questioned their ability to keep track of their three rowdy preteens while trying to raise a baby. Sneaking out of the house at the ages of eight, ten, and twelve was not something my father had fathomed the night his wife went into labor with their youngest. Sue, Danny, and I, however, saw it as an opportunity.

It was the summer of 1978. The gang was trying desperately to find ways to prolong the beautiful, July evening when Dad rushed my mom to the hospital. I reminded everyone that Mr. Reed had been nagging us all school year about standing in his yard while we waited for the bus. He worried we would crush his precious grass that he manicured so diligently every Saturday morning. It was evil that the school district required the kids to line up on a concrete slab embedded into the front lawn of the only habitat on Kenyon devoid of children, as we waited for Pete the bus driver to fetch us each morning.

It may have been my idea, but it didn't take much to convince the others to join me in compensating Mr. Reed for his disdain towards children. Jimmy, Karlene, and Sandy went home to dress in black clothes and prepare to sneak out of the house after dark. We would all meet on the golf course near the outhouse and plan the details of our reckoning on Old Mr. Reed.

We knew Dad's habits well enough to know that after he had returned from the hospital he would retire to his den and we would be on our own. The perfect chance to sneak out of the house seemed to be the first thought that passed through my ten-year-old mind.

Gathering outside the concrete outhouse on the golf course, not far from our target, we devised a plan. We would quietly sneak through the small field and jump over the narrow creek separating the homes on Kenyon from the golf course, hiding behind bushes until we reached the Reed's backyard. Our pact was that no one could speak, laugh, or make any noise. Everyone would surround the cement porch, squatting to avoid being seen.

We thought we were stealth, sneaking up on the small, yellow house occupied by a retired couple as if we were a Green Beret team. Sue and Sandy hid behind a bush while Danny and Jimmy went first. Karlene and I were close behind the boys, more than ready to cause mayhem.

Once we were in place surrounding the front door, we whispered, *"one, two, three"* and began banging on the brown metal screen door with all our might. After about five pounds each, we planned to run back where we came from, we only wanted to create enough noise to scare the geezer from his slumber. That's when our plan failed us.

The door flew open on our third knock and Mr. Reed, with his bulging belly straddled by overstretched suspenders, was looming in the doorway with a rifle. He swiftly reached down with his free hand to grab the nearest child, and my eight-year-old brother was closest to his grasp. The old man yanked Danny by the wrist and lifted him in the air like a rag doll. We screamed as one. The frightened look on Danny's face was the last thing we had seen before the door slammed and our little brother became a kidnapping victim of this greasy-haired ogre who brandished a gun to minors.

Afraid to confront a psycho with a rifle, we decided to run home and solicit help from an adult. Sue, Karlene, Jimmy, Sandy, and I ran as fast as our legs could carry us across the backyard, over the creek, and through the golf course. Nearly out of breath, we decided Jimmy's house was the best option to convene since we were sure the other parents were still awake.

Aunt Leanne maintained a luscious garden that stretched a third of the length of her property bordering on the Espinosa's yard. Exhausted and hurried when we reached my cousin's backyard, a few of us took a shortcut through her garden stomping on her precious plants in our rush to save Danny. I never saw the rusty remnants of a steel pole protruding from the ground that long ago supported an old swing set, but was now used as a stake to bear tomato plants in the spring.

I was wearing jeans and didn't realize the damage it had done to my shin when I felt the impact of running straight into the pole and fell to the ground. My dear sister and friends did not miss the opportunity to laugh at me because I tumbled. I jumped up quickly and casually asked Jimmy if I could use his bathroom. He reminded me to be quiet, we didn't want to wake his family.

The old farmhouse was familiar, but the Espinosa's upgraded every room of the house, only improving on the charm. I snuck into the bathroom on the immediate right. I knew their parents slept on the upper floor, and the walls were thick, I still closed the door gently and tiptoed across the linoleum floor until I reached the vanity near the open window.

Carefully lifting my injured, right leg onto the countertop, I dreaded what I was about to see. I easily pulled the pant leg of my bell bottom jeans over my knee, my stomach fell as I discovered the bloody inside of my shin and the bone that sat not far below the surface. I must have been in shock, my first thought was how much it resembled a slice of pizza after removing the cheese, and all that was left was the bumpy crust and remnants of tomato sauce. My love of pizza did not stop me from screaming. I shrieked until I woke up the entire Espinosa household.

Once Jimmy's parents saw the degree of my wound and learned of Danny's kidnapping, they had no choice but to call my dad. The sergeant arrived with hat in hand to retrieve his daughters and acknowledge the news of his son's kidnapping. Before freeing Danny, my father wanted to understand the details of the evening and how my brother went missing when he thought we were sleeping. I tried to play the pity card and wept at the same time I pointed at my bleeding leg, gently reminding him I needed immediate medical attention.

Sue chose the preteen attitude route and scowled at him, huddling on our twin beds as he berated us for our unruly behavior. We didn't realize the approach we were taking was the last thing our dad wanted from his eldest daughters until we saw the trophies, perfume bottles, and jewelry soaring across the room. He pushed Sue's dresser to the ground, hurling her teenage clutter to the floor and blocking our path to the exit before slamming the door and storming down the hall.

28

I thought I'd give Dad a few minutes to cool off before I imagined he would return to physically pick me up and drive me to the Massillon ER. Instead, I heard the front door slam and the tires of his pickup truck peeling out of the driveway. Sue and I had hoped he was at least retrieving Danny. The pain in my leg was masked by the adrenaline rushing through my body, but I was eager to have it sewn back together.

As I sat on the bed, covering the wound with the bloody towel the Espinosa's insisted I keep, Sue put the dresser back in place. We both regretted putting our little brother in this situation and imagined how terrified he must be. About fifteen minutes later, we were thrilled to see the scared, little guy walk through our bedroom door but sad to see his tear-stained cheeks.

Danny assured us he was fine, but he was clearly traumatized by the frightening ordeal. Later, he replayed the interaction with his kidnapper and the unpleasant humiliation our law-abiding father experienced that night. The intimidating, old man scolded Danny on behalf of all of us, as my brother sat shaking in a living room chair, a wintergreen scent wafting through the stuffy house. Dad stood in the doorway with his head bowed, repeatedly apologizing for the disruption his children caused. He glared across the room shooting daggers with his eyes at his only son. Mr. Reed handed my brother over as Dad guaranteed his elderly neighbor that this behavior would *never* happen again.

When I heard the engine still roaring, I hobbled to the driveway and jumped into the truck to take Danny's seat. He assumed my former position and stretched out on my bed near Sue, understandably not wanting to be alone. Our big sister chose to stay home and console our shaken little brother instead of riding along to the hospital. Smart girl. I, on the other hand, had no choice but to endure my father's surly mood and admonishment on the drive to the Massillon ER before I surrendered myself to the medical staff on-duty.

They shaved a patch of hair from my leg, shot a numbing agent into my shin with a long needle, and continued to suture twenty-five stitches to close the gaping hole. During the excitement, my dad visited Mom two floors above in the maternity ward. It was past visiting hours, so he explained the situation to the nurse behind the desk. That early July evening, we set a record when three Gossage's were patients at the Massillon Hospital at the same time.

Eden

The Kimmensville kids were familiar with the uniqueness of our parent's calls across the terrain, and we ran home when beckoned. My mom whistled by forming a circle with her thumb and forefinger between her lips and blowing twice, "*Phweeeeet, Phweet.*" Ronnie folded his tongue back with his first two fingers to form his distinctive shriek. Aunt Leanne shook a brass cowbell she bought in Amish country to call for my cousins. Jimmy's dad just cupped his hands around his mouth and yelled deep and loud, "*Jiiimmmeeeerrrrrr.*" Until our parents summoned us, we had the freedom to explore the great outdoors with our comrades from sunrise to sunset. It was a glorious time, a magnificent place to grow up.

The almost fictional perfection of our childhood and the cohesive community we formed on the back nine of my grandfather's golf course is what made our lives feel like our own private paradise. The setting was idyllic. There were no other neighbors within earshot to disturb. Our parents allowed us to run up and down the street banging pots and pans every New Year's Eve at midnight. No one seemed to mind. We were all family.

On sunny but rainy afternoons, rainbows straddled the corn field across the street from our homes. A tactic to get us out of the house following a storm, Mom convinced us to look for the treasure and leprechaun at the end. We ran through the maze of stalks in search of the pot of gold, never finding the prize but always enjoying the hunt.

The apple orchard doubled as a playground for us kids and every fall it supplied the neighborhood with homemade apple cider. Another cherished haunt was the weeping willow tree by the pond on the golf course. We rested under the umbrella of leaves during hot summer days to shade ourselves while we fished, never catching one, but enjoying the calmness

31

of the water and the silence between us. In the winter, we ice skated on the frozen pond and made snow angels all over the course.

On calm summer evenings, fireflies lit up the golf course like an airport runway. We peacefully watched the sporadic, yellow sparkles against the black sky. Other times we joined them. They hovered at our height, quickly climbing as we zipped through the sea of blinking bugs with our arms extended like airplanes. When we tired of flying with them, we cupped our hands and captured as many of the glowing, brown beetles as we could hold. They vanished when their glow extinguished, only to reappear a few feet away. We lunged from one flicker to the next, trying to imprison them while they were briefly visible. Observing the leathery wings of our incarcerated fireflies and noticing they only blinked from their rear ends, Danny giggled and nicknamed them "lightning butts."

Mom shared a childhood story with us about capturing lightning bugs. Of course, we took her scheme to the next level. The neighborhood kids huddled on our concrete stoop and placed the dazed insects in a glass jar. Our victims were dizzy and confused by the commotion, never trying to escape their captivity. They would have if they knew we were about to make glow-in-the-dark jewelry out of their hinds.

Timing was everything when separating the shining ends from the torso. We had to dissect the insect when the abdomen was lit. Otherwise, you ended up with a dud. We quickly mastered the skill of firefly jewelry making.

At first, we just made rings. Then we moved onto constructing bracelets, and eventually, necklaces. Regardless of how many pieces we made, the glowing bugs appeared in droves. Our supply chain was endless. The little critters had the destiny to end up as accessories. Their bodies secured themselves together when we joined the lighted extremities, no additional supplies needed for our upcoming fashion show. Our parents wore awkward expressions as we sauntered down the

32

driveway wearing our glowing jewelry, concerned about our lack of empathy towards living creatures.

The firefly massacres ended after we noticed the putrid smell it left on our skin. We scrubbed our fingers raw and still noticed the pungent odor the following day. It never occurred to us the foul-smelling pheromones were protection from predators. We all agreed to observe our beautiful, twinkling friends from afar and buy our baubles at the mall.

The apple orchard wasn't as fortunate. Directly behind the barn stood two rows of trees, all red, except for one yellow sapling. The trees grew on the former farmland, decades before my grandpa turned it into a golf course. They were now sturdy and broad enough to hold a few kids each.

One of our favorite ways to pass the time was to lie in a shaded apple tree on a warm afternoon. We often spotted a robin's nest nestled in the branches and admired the delicate, blue eggs in awe, never touching them. Danny waited patiently and collected the discarded powder blue shells after the babies hatched. He carried them home and carefully arranged them on his dresser.

We decided during a Kimmensville Club meeting to build a tree house in the largest apple tree. The thick trunk split into three sprawling boughs, smaller branches jutting from every limb. By the time we adopted it, the tree was at least two stories high. We brought nails, hammers, rope, a bucket, scraps of rug, and fabric. Peat moss, scraped from the base of the damp trunks supplemented the carpet.

We all claimed a spot on the tree and constructed our individual "rooms." Danny and Jimmy nailed square pieces of carpeting and moss to the branches, functioning as pillows. The girls hung curtains using scraps of fabric, providing privacy for our abodes. The bucket and rope were used to lift supplies that we needed from below. One person would be relegated to fetch for the gang while someone else pulled the cord.

Satisfied, we lounged in our new dwelling, stared at the sky, and chatted about the day's events like the Walton kids hollering from their bedrooms. However, our dream to meet there each day was short-lived.

Mom's cousin, the manager of the Elms, discovered our creation the next morning. He saw in the distance what appeared to be a homeless camp in the middle of his golf course. Mismatched curtains hung from the branches, a plastic bucket dangled from the rope. As his golf cart approached the cluster of trees, he knew we must have been the architects of this shanty. Mark Sweany grabbed a hammer from the back of his cart and began deconstructing our tree house. He was undoubtedly shaking his head and cursing his family the entire time.

Mark called my mom and ranted about cleaning up our mess. He also presumed that we damaged the old tree. Sue, Danny, and I ran to the orchard and confirmed the harrowing call. Everything was gone. Our efforts and dreams of lackadaisical afternoons in the tree house were shattered. We didn't like to think we injured our giant friend and doubted a few nails would take down the beast.

Thankfully, the tree survived and so did our creativity. After that episode, we nicknamed our mom's cousin, Weany. It wouldn't be our last interaction with the golf course manager and future heir to the Elms dynasty.

The red barn behind the farmhouse held a trove of hidden treasures that the parents preferred we left alone. The temptation was too strong. Sue, Danny, Jimmy, and I spent an entire day constructing a go-kart from golf push carts we found on the ground floor. They were mostly broken, just a few were still intact. We used the parts and invented a crude engineless go-kart. It only worked going downhill, and our running shoes acted as the breaks. Otherwise, it was impressive. Before we took it for a spin, Mom snapped a picture with her new Kodak Instamatic to capture the moment.

The ride was unwieldy without a steering wheel. I veered off the road and settled in a ditch, a few times. We had a blast as we rode down the hill all afternoon and pushed the cart back up for the next rider. The go-kart excitement ended when the back wheels finally separated from the frame. We didn't have the energy to build another one. It was fun while it lasted and we were proud that we used our imagination and teamwork to get it done, two competencies the kids on the street were never lacking.

A clever idea was hatched during a torrential summer downpour. We noticed that a stream resembling a gigantic water slide was forming at the bottom of the hill behind our house. Lightning often accompanied the rain clouds in Ohio. It was fascinating to witness the electrifying flashes touch the flat course. The grass sizzled like bacon in a frying pan when a bolt made contact with the wet lawn. If we saw thunder or lightning, we observed nature through the windows. When there was only rain, we ran around with our friends in the showers until we shivered and voted to go home and take warm baths.

There was no lightning the day we discovered the natural water slide forming on the course. We called the neighborhood kids, and everyone met at our house, shoeless and dressed in old shirts and shorts. Grass stains were inevitable as we slid across the flooded course.

The stream started outside Karlene's backyard and ran parallel to the twenty-fifth fairway, almost reaching the Sweany house. Our cousins Mike and Patrick even joined in the fun. We didn't see much of Mark's boys. Mike was kind of quiet, and Patrick spent most of his time spinning his dad's albums and picking on his guitar.

Danny had sprinted a few yards before he dove in the air, hands clasped above his head. He landed flat on his belly, lifted his chin and feet into the air, and slid like a slippery seal. We all laughed and screamed as we sailed back and forth. We held contests to determine who coasted the furthest. Every kid in the neighborhood was trembling, our lips turned purple. Covered in mud, blades of grass sticking to our skin and jutting out of our hair, we were never happier.

On dryer days, the slope behind our house was just steep and long enough to roll down. Lying on our sides, we spun down the hill, coasting to a dizzy stop at the twenty-fourth green. We stumbled and fell when we tried to stand. As we aged, our need for speed escalated. Sue suggested using my dad's fifty-five-gallon steel drum, which he used to burn garbage. We found our new vessel and rolled it to the golf course.

The interior was caked with reddish-orange colored rust from the high temperatures of the fires. The rainfall that collected inside only added to the deterioration. Danny grabbed an old hoodie and knit hat. We took turns putting them on before we climbed into the oxidized barrel. The group of us laid the drum on its side and gripped it tightly to allow the passenger to crawl in, feet first. The rider braced their body against the cavity and gave the thumbs-up sign. The rest of us pushed the barrel from behind, running as fast as we could. When it reached the incline, we let gravity take the wheel.

After the drum had settled at the bottom of the hill, inches from the green, the giddy rider crawled from the canister and staggered around the course like a drunk, eventually falling from the spiraling journey. We spent hours rolling down, laughing at each other, and then pushing the barrel back up the hill. Satisfied the number of turns was even, we agreed on an activity that didn't make our heads spin. Jimmy suggested fishing at the pond, giving our noggins a chance to rest.

Our fathers only allowed us to use their fishing rods when they were with us. Borrowing a tip from a Saturday morning cartoon, we fashioned poles from tree branches and white thread with large safety pins tied to the end. We didn't worry about bringing the bait. We used the worms and bugs we found slithering around the vegetation at the pond. No one seemed to care that we never caught anything. It was an excuse to do nothing for a couple of hours except hang out with our friends.

Sitting beneath the canopy of the weeping willow tree made me feel safe and protected. I loved its majestic beauty. The long branches reached the ground and slowly swept the grass in the soft breeze. The leaves concealed us behind the swinging curtain, cool and damp inside, a natural air conditioner in the summer. We rested under it as we fished the afternoon away, hypnotized by the swaying of the branches.

There was a lack of commotion around our homemade fishing rods, so we agreed to head to the orchard. As we rounded the pond, we spotted our catch. The ugly catfish had thick whiskers poking from its face, dark brown spots covered the slimy body. The fish was already out of the water, lying on the ground waiting for us to take him home. Dad would be so happy. I imagined he would use his sharp silver hunting knife to carefully slice it up before frying it in a pan on the stove.

Things didn't go as planned. We took the time to hook the dead fish to the safety-pin and proudly presented our smelly catch, dangling from the sewing thread, pieces of grass stuck to its body. My sportsman father knew right away the catch was not fresh. We thought it was quite considerate of us to drag the dead fish across the golf course and were a bit insulted.

Instead of carving it up for supper, he told us to dispose of it somewhere far away, so he didn't have to smell the *damn* thing. We chose the cornfield as the final resting place and heaved the catfish between the stalks. Shaking our heads in dismay, we asked each other, "So, what do you wanna' do now?"

Aunt Leanne quelled some of our boredom by hosting the occasional Craft Day on weekend afternoons. I loved Craft Day at Leanne's. She greeted us at the door with an apron tied around her tall, thin frame. The dining room table was carefully protected, identical supplies were perfectly arranged on each place mat. She always planned ahead and had everything we needed for the activity that day. Leanne also introduced us to peanut butter and banana wheat bread sandwiches, always with a drizzle of honey. This type of fare was absent in my household, much too healthy.

I loved my mom and the fact that she thrived on mishaps, messes, and unplanned afternoons that always amounted to a tremendous amount of fun. Days with Leanne were structured and calm, something I also appreciated. Mom didn't enjoy cooking or cleaning; you would never catch her wearing an apron. We grew up consuming processed lunch meat, white bread, pop, baked goods, fast food, and potato chips in quantities that would make you believe the apocalypse was approaching. The food was endless. The rules and boundaries around nutrition were non-existent.

We often heard the threat, *"If you eat everything now, there will be nothing left for your school lunches!"* Regardless of how much we consumed, there was always a meal waiting for me in my *Scooby Doo* lunch pail. Mom usually made me bologna sandwiches topped with ketchup that leaked through the white bread, resembling a dead body that was stabbed and stuffed into a plastic bag. She made up for it by throwing in a bag of Fritos, a package of Twinkies, or a Hostess Apple Pie on special occasions.

Mom was many things, but she was not an artisan. I appreciated Aunt Leanne living next door. The calligraphy she taught us came in handy when I inscribed the envelopes for my wedding invitations. I passed this skill onto my daughter so she could recreate the Constitution of the U.S. on a piece of parchment paper for a school project. Leanne taught us patience and creativity. She showed us how to use our hands and our imagination to concoct whatever we wanted. It's not a surprise Colleen became such a talented artist. Leanne was an inspiration. She also never hesitated to yell at us from an open window when she became aware of our mischief. The kids were acutely aware of her vigilance. We avoided Leanne when our intentions were not good.

Weany was the most important adult to watch out for when we were on the golf course, which was most of the time. We didn't realize the cause of our strained relationship was due to the havoc we were wreaking on the Elms. We just thought he didn't like us. I realize now he was maintaining the integrity of the course our grandfather built. We sure didn't make it easy for him.

Our shenanigans were mostly harmless, but they certainly weren't honest. Danny, Jimmy, and I started snatching the golf balls that landed near our backyard. We noticed the golfers were hidden behind the apple orchard when they played the twenty-fourth fairway. If we couldn't see them, then they wouldn't spot us running up the slope from our backyard and grabbing the balls. We scampered back to the house and watched their reactions from my bedroom window. Eventually, the golfers gave up searching, and after a few expletives threw down another ball and took a one-stroke penalty.

We carried our stash in the front of our T-shirts to the ball washer near the pond so our parents wouldn't see us. The boys took turns pumping the handle until the golf balls sparkled. I used the towel hanging from the chain to dry them and scrape off the remaining marks and grass stains. Most of the balls could pass as new, and the twenty-five-cent price tag was a hit with the men, but we worried we would be caught. Weany wasn't aware we were reselling stolen balls to his golfers until we got greedy.

We moved on to driving range golf balls because they were much easier to collect. We asked each other as we walked home from the swimming pool, "Why hadn't we thought of this idea earlier?" Danny and Jimmy discreetly nabbed balls that landed near the tree line, I did cartwheels grabbing a ball in each hand and shoving them in my pockets. The range balls had a bright red stripe around the center. Otherwise, they looked like the ones that had made us some decent pocket change. After shining them in the ball washer, we approached a golfer with our sales pitch. He laughed at us and pointed out our error. I'm sure he's the guy that ratted us out.

Weany wasn't pleased with us, but he wasn't as angry as the time Sue parted the hair of a golfer with an arrow. Danny and I were shooting our new bows at some bales of hay in the backyard when Sue asked if she could join us. She aimed high, released the string, and the arrow soared above the target, into the course. We didn't see the golfer until he yelled at us to stop shooting at him. We waited for the foursome to pass before we showed Sue how to accurately aim for the target.

When the skittish golfer returned to the clubhouse, he reported the near fatality to the manager. Weany knew which family had weapon-wielding kids on the back nine. He stormed across the golf course, headed directly for our house.

Our cousin arrived with spit flying from his mouth. He admonished us while he grabbed the arrows lying on the ground. He even snatched the few that hit the target and left with all of them. Sue, Danny, and I went inside and told Dad about our confiscated property, we just omitted *why* they were taken. Dad was pissed off at his relative through marriage, marched to his home, and took back the arrows he found lying in their garage.

Weany didn't seem to mind when we tore across the course on our mini bikes or played a neighborhood game of kickball as the sun was setting. There were so many conflicts with the Kimmensville Club, he wisely chose his battles. Weany did support the apple cider venture and always profited with several extra gallons for his generosity. It was fun being a part of the Amish cider-making operation until I saw the entire process and swore off apple cider.

The harvest was always pre-planned and announced to every household in Kimmensville. The message was to meet in the orchard with your pickup trucks, kids, and empty plastic two-gallon jugs. We scurried up every tree and shook the branches to free the delicious fruit from their stems. The stubborn apples had to be yanked from their shaft by hand, which required the kids to hug the branches as we scooted to the end. When the bed of each truck held its capacity of apples, the driver headed southwest with a few kids in tow to the processing center in Amish Country.

The operation was archaic, but I didn't expect the natural flavorings that ended up in the jugs of frothy, brown juice. Our fathers backed their trucks into the loading dock and released the back doors. The apples spilled out and rolled across a large square grate. After the fruit had settled on the platform, I expected some type of shower that would rinse the grime and bugs off of the ingredients that were about to become our fruit drink.

Instead, an identical sized wooden plank was slowly lowered on top of the crowded apples. It squeezed them until the dirty juice poured freely into a funnel positioned below the grate. The stream of cider flowed directly into our jugs lined up beneath the operation.

In future years, I didn't mind gathering apples for the cider production. It was always a fun afternoon. I just politely declined any offers for a mug of the unfiltered bug juice. The neighborhood families split the jugs of cider and enjoyed them throughout the fall. Ronnie always stashed a few too long on purpose, fermenting them until they became hard liquor.

The unforgettable memories were not all ours. Our parents also reminisce about the days they spent living on the golf course and the friendships they built. I'm sure even Weany would concede that we created an incredible community, although a little unwieldy at times. We genuinely had the perfect world growing up on the Elms Golf Course.

Mother Goose and Her Goslings

Mom was the center of our world and known to every child she met as Mother Goose. Our fun-loving parent did not work outside of the home but decided even house cleaning came second to playing with us. She always had time for her own children, as well as any kid in the neighborhood or school that needed her. We all felt cherished when my mom was around.

She allowed us to invite a few kids when we went to the grocery store, church on Sundays, even to our doctor appointments. We knew we could talk Mom into stopping at Crème Buffet for soft serve ice cream or McDonald's for hot apple pies. We expressed our gratitude with hugs and kisses, followed up by written notes. Sometimes, Danny, Colleen, and I painted her murals on broken pieces of slate that we found in the barn. As much as we treasured her, not unlike my dad, we often took full advantage of her generosity and affection.

My parents were complete opposites in every way. In 1963, the summer before their senior year of high school, they met at the Elms. Grandpa Howard's younger sister, Margaret, became his business partner, and they expanded the golf course by adding a swimming pool and tennis courts. The property was beautiful and attracted plenty of families from Massillon every summer to keep the business flourishing. While Mom spent her summer swimming with her siblings, Grandpa hired Dad to work as a lifeguard.

Despite her younger sister's pleas, my parents began dating. Judi didn't think Dad showed my mom enough respect. One evening, to avoid getting his car dirty he asked her to walk to the end of her unpaved street for their date. She did. The icing on the cake for my aunt was the night he invited Mom to the movies and met her in the lobby, past the ticket agent.

On New Year's Eve, against her sister's urging and their better judgment, they were married at nineteen. As children, we imagined they were romantics in love, getting married so young on such an exciting and celebratory night. To our disappointment, we learned that Dad wanted the marriage tax break since they were expecting the arrival of my sister. It took us until our preteens to figure out Mom was three months pregnant with little Sue-Sue when they wed and spent their honeymoon in Niagara Falls.

Like many young fathers, my dad saw the military as an opportunity to support his family and travel around the world. He had joined the Army before Sue turned one, the same time they found out Mom was pregnant with me.

She was a small-town girl with no experience traveling outside of her comfort zone, yet Mom quickly adapted. She lived on the U.S. Army base in Büdingen, Germany where she raised Sue without her family support system. Dad worked all day and occasionally drove their only car for week-long maneuvers.

The winter of 1967, Mom was nine months pregnant with me, had a toddler in tow, and was determined to mail Christmas cards to her family and friends back home. Dad had driven the car to a military drill, so she walked miles over snow-covered cobblestone roads to the Post Office. On warmer days, the military moms pushed their strollers, stopping at local cafés for coffee and brötchen. She felt so cosmopolitan walking to the small markets to do her daily shopping.

The afternoon she was expecting me at any moment, she felt anything but sophisticated. Mom hobbled home on swollen ankles from her quest and called the hospital to tell them she was in labor. An inept military driver responded to her plea but neglected to grab her overnight bag sitting near the front door. He escorted my mother to his car and sped us over more cobblestone roads to the Ninety-Seventy General Hospital in Frankfurt, Germany where she gave birth to me within two hours of arriving.

Mom didn't know anyone on base well enough to expect a visit, and Dad was still deployed. No one to bring our things, Mom spent three lonely days at the hospital and left in the same clothes she arrived in. Instead of donning the pink and white dress with a matching bonnet she picked out for me, I was presented to the world swaddled in a military issued T-shirt with *U.S. ARMY* stenciled across my chest.

A neighbor, Mrs. Frotscher, became the babysitter for us Army brats in the building and my mom's best friend. Mom was grateful for her new companion and was thrilled when her friend taught Sue to speak German. At first, my parents thought it was adorable when their bilingual toddler rattled off her numbers and colors in both dialects. They didn't realize Sue would prefer the guttural vocabulary of our caretaker to the language spoken by the rest of her family.

One day, an English-speaking friend named Sophie tended to my three-year-old sister and me. Sue walked around the apartment yelling the German word, "*puppe!*" Sophie placed her on the toilet. She didn't understand why my sister continued to blubber about poop, nothing left her bowel. Sue's sobs from the bathroom grew louder and even more dramatic as the day progressed, "*Puppe!! Puppe!!!*" My parents returned home to a hysterical toddler and frazzled babysitter. My mom explained to Sophie that puppe is the German translation for a doll, and then found Sue's favorite toy.

In March of 1969, Mom's European experience ended abruptly. A letter arrived from Grandma Alice asking my mom to return home to her ailing father. Mom adored her generous and loving dad and never hesitated as she packed our bags. Our father joined us after his deployment, but it was too late for Dad. Grandpa died a week after we had arrived.

My grandpa's legacy still thrives in the family and community today. I love the stories that circulate about the Catholic priests who never paid for a round of golf or the minorities who were welcomed by my grandfather without prejudice when other courses denied them entrance. I was less than two years old, but it was enough time for my darling grandpa to fondly nickname me Two Ton. Unfortunately, it was a moniker that did not pass with him.

Grandpa Howard's death was incredibly hard for my mom. She was expecting her third child that fall and was heartbroken that her father would never meet Danny. My parents were barely twenty-five when they settled into the farmhouse on the golf course with a toddler and two children in diapers. While my dad began his career as a trooper with the Ohio State Highway Patrol, Mom had her hands full chasing the three of us around the property.

If we weren't outside, the kids on the block typically played in our house. Mom had very few rules and encouraged us to enjoy ourselves. She didn't get upset when we broke things or panic when we hurt ourselves. She convinced us that if our injuries didn't kill us, they would make us stronger, except for the time Sue and I slammed Danny's pinky finger in a door. Mom dropped the phone and rushed Danny to the ER where the doctors reconnected the top of his finger, although a little lopsided.

Danny was a sensitive, little man who loved our mother more than anything else in the world. My brother would tell her he wanted to marry her when he grew up, as he hugged her and covered her cheeks with kisses. Mom smiled, hugged him back, and glowed in the attention.

Our mom had beautiful, olive skin and thick, black, silky hair that she wore in ponytails, resembling Pocahontas. Danny would stroke her long mane and vow to buy her a red dress and new carpet when he landed his first job. I am sure he would have followed through with his promises if he could have.

When he attended kindergarten, Danny tenderly picked dandelions in the schoolyard. He presented the flowers to our mom, reminding her how much he loved her. The flowers were always wilted, but Mom filled a small glass with cold water and proudly displayed her spray on the kitchen table. Danny grinned, convinced his thoughtfulness made her happy. It always did. He was an incredibly compassionate and empathetic young man, his love extending to animals. My brother never finished an episode of *Lassie* without sobbing.

When he was five, Danny talked Mom into adopting a free puppy we found advertised in the classified section of the *Massillon Independent*. "It says the dog is part-*beagle*," he pleaded. Beagles were our dad's favorite breed. He longed for a sidekick to join him on hunting trips, so we threw that in for good measure. Mom caved in and suggested we surprise Dad with the part-beagle puppy for Christmas. She called the number in the ad before we all piled into the car and headed out to meet the remaining litter.

Sue, Danny, and I laid eyes on the runt and instantly fell in love, we knew this dog would be ours. She had black fur, light brown spots, and white rings circled her dark eyes. The puppy fell down when she tried to run, she was perfect. We instantly forgot about finding a hunting dog for our father and bonded with the awkward pup.

We surprised Dad that night with his "Christmas present." He looked at the excited puppy, knitted his brows, and said, "What *is* it?" Mom was shocked, "It's a *beagle*, Steve!" Dad laughed and assured her in his cynical tone, it was *not* a beagle. Mom admitted it was actually bred with another of his favorite dogs, a German Shepherd. He shook his head and told us three anxious kids that we could have the puppy. Since that was our plan, it worked out well for us. We lovingly named our new puppy Schatzi, our translation of the word sweetie in German.

When I was ten and Danny was eight years old, Dad took us hunting in Virginia with a goal to bring home our Thanksgiving dinner. He hoped his son would share his passion, not realizing my brother's love for animals would prevent him from shooting a living creature. The Virginia episode was the beginning and end of the hunting expeditions for my brother and me.

We pitched our tent on the land his friend owned, among the acres of tranquil, rolling green hills peppered with pine trees. Dad introduced us to Mr. and Mrs. Clark before we drove into town for supplies at the general store, which could have doubled as the set of Ike's General Mercantile on *The Waltons*. Danny and I ran through the aisles calling each other "John-Boy" and "Mary Ellen."

I refused to use the great outdoors as a latrine, so I visited the Clark's house more often than the boys. Whenever I knocked, she let me sneak in to use their modern-day toilet. One late night trip back to our campground, I swore I spotted Bigfoot and sprinted up the hill to our tent. Between gasps, I reported the sighting to my camping partners. Dad seriously doubted me. He thought I was overly dramatic, assured me it was a shadow, and quickly dismissed my claim. Eyes as wide as saucers, my brother wasn't so sure. Dad didn't know we had just watched "The Secret of Bigfoot" episode of Danny's favorite show, *The Six Million Dollar Man*. Neither of us slept that night.

Each morning, our hostess prepared a hearty breakfast for my dad, brother, and me. We ate hungrily while the roaring fire warmed our bones. After sleeping an inch off of the frozen ground with only the thin nylon tent shielding our heads, we needed the heat.

I had never experienced such an amazing breakfast: homemade Belgian waffles with fruit jam, thick slices of bacon, and real maple syrup. In between bites, we complimented Mrs. Clark. Although we didn't need any urging, the missus encouraged us to have second helpings. She reminded us that we had a long day of walking ahead of us with just the snacks in our coats until we returned for dinner. Danny and I each grabbed another piece of bacon.

The fowl Danny was "hunting" were oblivious to the weapon pointed in their direction. A massive flock of wild turkeys pecked the spacious, green hill as Danny aimed the shotgun at them, and froze. One of us made a noise, probably me. Turkeys have exceptional eyesight and hearing, so they quickly dispersed before Dad was able to grab the rifle from Danny and get a shot off.

Our dad wasn't pleased with Danny's faint heart and my interference. Eventually, he shot a bird for our Thanksgiving bounty, but Danny and I couldn't eat it. Much to my father's dismay, that year we feasted on stuffing, mashed potatoes, and pecan pie.

Dad snapped a photo of me holding the dead bird by the legs. Danny had refused to be a part of it. Then, he used his kill as a learning opportunity and demonstrated how to clean a turkey. He stressed the importance of working quickly, so the meat doesn't spoil. After removing the bird's intestines, Dad sliced open the stomach to show us a sack of small pebbles. He said turkeys don't have teeth to chew their food, so they intentionally eat stones to help digest their meal.

I appreciated the anatomy lesson, but after our breakfast banquet, seeing it was more than my stomach could handle. I excused myself and hiked to the cabin for a break. My dad found me an hour later reclining in the living room chair chatting it up with Mrs. Clark in front of the blistering fire.

I always thought it was our choice to forgo future hunting trips with our father. More than likely, it was a mutual decision.

Dad hunted all over North America, including a month in the Yukon Territory. He and his partners hired local Native American guides with horses for their trek into the Canadian wilderness. We rode along with Mom when his flight was due to arrive at the Cleveland Airport, expecting Dad to have a few gifts for us.

No one anticipated the extra luggage he was hauling. He pushed a cart with several long, bulging, plastic bags that resembled body bags. We soon discovered that's exactly what they were, for dead animals. Between the carcasses and the full beard, we were a little standoffish when he lunged to hug his family. The handmade Eskimo jewelry and wallets he brought us compensated for the corpses in the trunk. Even my mom forgave him when she saw the bottle of Chanel No. 5 he bought her at the Duty-Free shop.

Mom attempted to cook whatever gamey meat he brought home. Numerous lifeless deer had hung from the wooden beams in our garage, their back feet bound by a thick rope. He skinned his catch to avoid extra taxidermy charges. The neighbor dogs clamored outside the closed garage door, sniffing and whining at the barricade. We peeked out of the kitchen door and watched our father use his silver hunting knife to remove the coats skillfully. When the blade dulled from overuse, he sharpened it on a piece of gritstone. A few days later, I recognized my dinner and opted for carbs.

The most common dead animal stored in our freezer was a deer. Unfortunately for all of us, venison was not an ingredient our mother ever mastered. Dad's paltry, government employee income was the sole means to support our expanding family and appetites, so he continued to hunt, and we survived on meals my mom poured from boxes and cans. After adding some sort of browned meat, she placed our supper next to a bowl of soggy, bland, faded produce. Vegetables never had a fair shot in our house.

Mom eventually realized her kids were not eating dinner when it consisted of "dead Bambi." She tried to hide the meat and even lied a few times when we asked her what she added to the mystery meal. Her worst idea was adding a can of Manwich Sloppy Joe sauce to sautéed, ground venison. The flavors from the sugary, red sauce did not mask the gamey taste of the meat as she had hoped--it only added to it. We all turned our noses up at the pungent grub and made a peanut butter and jelly sandwich for dinner.

Dad made a few decent meals for us that didn't involve venison, but because of his schedule, they were few and far between. After my exposure to dead animals, and my mother's attempt at cooking them, I settled for processed food. Sue, Danny, and I learned to cook for ourselves, although our meals were not much of an improvement. We could usually count on a Chef Boyardee pizza kit in our cupboard but never had any decent toppings. My siblings and I settled for American cheese slices and "pepperonis," which we made by punching circles into bologna slices using the lid of a ketchup bottle.

My family never had much money, but we felt comfortable living on the golf course. Through example, Mom taught us to be grateful for what we had. It didn't always rub off, but she was an encouraging role model. Mom believed the essentials for a happy life were the simple things; she indulged us in all of them. Even today, she tries to instill these same values in her grandchildren.

She also taught us to laugh at ourselves and encouraged a sense of humor. I fondly recall the afternoon Mom took all of us kids to the movies to see *Grease*. We enjoyed the soundtrack so much we stopped at Kmart on the way home so Mom could buy us the album. She joined us as we bounced around the living room singing *Greased Lightnin'*, *We Go Together*, and *Look at Me, I'm Sandra Dee*.

51

We relentlessly performed for our mom and each other. Danny was the most entertaining. We laughed until we cried watching his various parodies and listening to his original songs. Other days, he almost drove us mad.

My little brother would stand tall in the living room, one hand on his chest, as confident as Luciano Pavarotti and belt out fictional opera songs. Always a string of noises instead of words. "*Laaaaaaa Meeeeeeee Keerrrrrrrrr Beeerrrrrrrrrrrr!!!*" Holding the last note, arms extended in the air until he ran out of breath. When he burst into a ballad in the middle of a *General Hospital* episode, which he often did, Sue and I would pummel him.

I am not sure how Mom put up with us some days, especially the times we embarrassed her in public, such as the spitball incidents. When she was confronted by a spit wad victim, Mom acted as if it was the first time we had assaulted a stranger with a soggy, paper bullet.

After talking Mom into stopping for fast food, we each grabbed a few extra plastic straws. They were conveniently covered in paper which transformed nicely into ammunition. We ripped a piece off and rolled it around on our tongue, adding just the right amount of spittle.

We started our attacks at the fast food restaurants, nailing oblivious patrons in the back of the head. Danny and Jimmy high-fived each other when a spitball lodged in someone's hair. The marks wearing shiny bomber jackets were clueless as they ate their burgers, chunks of wet paper stuck to the satin.

We were covert, but someone eventually felt the impact of the slimy ball and yelled at my mom. The usual advice they gave her was to discipline her kids. Mom always agreed with the stranger and expressed remorse. Then, she scolded us, "You kids. I didn't know you were doing that! Stop it!!"

We all laughed as we hopped into the car and continued our war on random Massillonians. Mom finally had to draw the line at shooting spit wads at moving vehicles. As we drove down Lincoln Way, Sue, Danny, Jimmy, and I, fully stocked with torpedoes, ambushed the car next to us.

As we idled at a red light, the stranger yelled, *"Hey Lady! You need to control your kids. They're shooting spit wads at my car!!"* and pointed to over twenty slobbery balls of paper stuck to her window. Once again, Mom feigned oblivion and apologized to the exasperated woman before she sped off at the green light. She joined in our laughter, and in case we tried it again, Mom casually lagged behind, careful not to pass the woman.

In spite of the ruckus we created, my mom continued to treat us to fast food. Dad refused to join us for a meal at any restaurant. He compared us to wild animals. His comment was more than justified, and he wasn't even aware of the majority of our dining experiences.

"The money is for a good cause," we urged. Mom dug out change from her purse, and we dropped it into the Jerry Lewis' Muscular Dystrophy Foundation collection box. It was a self-service model, so we each grabbed a latex balloon with a McDonald logo from the bowl and secured it to the valve on the helium tank. After inflating our balloons, we twisted the neck to contain the gas but didn't tie them. We giggled as we returned to our seats. Exhaling all of the air from our lungs, we quickly inhaled helium from the balloons, filling our developing organs with the inert gas.

Our favorite parody was to impersonate the Munchkins from the *Wizard of Oz* singing *Welcome to Munchkinland*. We scrapped the bottom of our shoes, hands deep in our pockets, lips puckered on one side while we sang in our new tiny voices:

We represent the *Lollypop Guild,*
The Lollypop Guild, The Lollypop Guild

And in the name of the *Lollypop Guild...*
We wish to welcome you to *Muchkinlaaaaannnnddd*

Regardless of the reactions we received, we performed our parodies at the restaurant, in the car, at home, and wherever we had an audience and helium. We were a rowdy group, but we also loved and cared for our little city.

Mom taught us to give back to the community and keep the places we frequented free of debris, so we spent many afternoons cleaning parks and playgrounds. We picked up garbage and pulled weeds, stuffing everything into plastic bags and putting them in the trunk. Only after our duties were completed, we ran for the swings and slides. To reward us, our beloved Mother Goose treated us to something gooey and delicious.

My ever-growing waistline was a testament to the abundance of sugar and salty food in our life. Dad planted a garden every year, as did every house on the street, so we had vegetables in our lives. We just preferred ice cream to carrots as a mid-day snack. We weren't the healthiest bunch.

Any neighborhood kid within earshot screamed when the Jingle Jim ice cream truck drove down Kenyon Road. He refused to drive down our pothole-ridden street, so we kept our ears open for the speakers blasting the catchy jingle. When we heard the music, we dropped everything, grabbed change from Mom's purse, and ran at top speed down Kimmens Road. We tracked him down barefoot, in our pajamas, whatever it took to catch Jingle Jim. I always ordered the frozen chocolate crunch bar while Sue preferred anything strawberry, and Danny usually went for the red, white, and blue Bomb Pop.

My mom was the queen of fun surprises and always made up a reason for our celebrations so we wouldn't think she was spoiling us. Her excuses ranged from the fact we earned good grades in school, did our chores, didn't fight during church, or just because she loved us.

Except for the days she took us to dinner at Ponderosa Steakhouse, no justification needed, we knew she was fighting with Dad over finances. Mom loved the fact Ponderosa took credit cards, Dad's mortal enemy, and Mom's best friend. As she backed out of the driveway, the three of us chanted, *"Du du – du - du - du - duuu, Charge!!"*

Sue, Danny, and I knew the drill when we entered the dark dining room. We each grabbed a plastic tray and slid the red platter down the counter, ordering hearty meals of sirloin steak smothered in sautéed mushrooms, corn on the cob, and baked potatoes with butter. If we had room, which my skinny sister amazingly always did, we finished off our feast with a slice of cheesecake drizzled with bright red cherry topping.

For a short time, Mom would forget about their argument and that they could not afford the meal she was enjoying with her kids. She would figure it out later.

In 1974, Mom planned a road trip to visit her mother and sisters in Florida. Dad wasn't able to take time off work, so Mom thought it would be fun to drive us three kids to St. Petersburg. We were five, seven, and nine years old. "Maybe we'll make a stop or two along the way to break up the drive for the kids," she told my dad.

Growing up with Mom was always an adventure, and this trip did not disappoint. She wanted us to have a memorable vacation. She would explain the credit card statement to Dad when we returned home.

Like many parents anxious to start a journey, Mom woke Sue and me up before the sunrise and Dad carried my sleeping brother to the car. The cold leather seats were lined with blankets and pillows so we could fall back asleep, sans seatbelts. The trunk of our pale-yellow Ford Torino was stuffed with our suitcases and a cooler full of snacks and drinks.

We slept until we heard Mom's excited voice, "Wake up, kids, we're *here!!*" I was blissfully surprised that I was able to sleep the entire way to the hotel Dad reserved for us in Tennessee.

Under the bright lights, a roller coaster and Ferris wheel came into vision. Kings Island was an amusement park in Cincinnati only 200 miles south. We were still in Ohio and had no intention of leaving the state that day.

Mom eased into a parking space as we jumped up and down on the car seats and screamed with excitement. She handed us each a bundle of clothes and shoes for the adventurous day. After ditching our pajamas and struggling into our shorts in the back seat, we set out for the park as the sun rose into the sky.

On the rides we were tall enough to enjoy, we were spun, jerked, splashed, and flipped. We gorged on cotton candy, snow cones, and hot dogs. When the park closed, we found a hotel nearby and ordered pizza delivered to our room.

As we waited for our greasy pie to arrive, Sue, Danny, and I jumped from one bed to the other in the outdated hotel room. Mom was talking to Dad on the phone, so she shushed us a few times, we were on a sugar rush and only dropped our shrieks by a decibel. Mom shared the news of our splendid day with Dad.

He was not pleased with her for spending so much money before she left Ohio, or that she missed the hotel reservation he made for us two states south. For a moment, we hung our heads in mock shame as she tried to justify the day to our father. Then we grabbed our Kings Island stuffed dogs we won playing games and went back to jumping on the beds, tossing the mascots along with us.

When the pizza arrived, we ate every slice, as well as the chips and pop she ordered on the side. Mom insisted we all take showers before going to bed. We begrudgingly obeyed but not without complaining about the scratchy towels and the soap that made us smell like an old lady.

The next morning, we checked out and stopped at the Cincinnati Zoo to visit the animals before we continued on our journey. We made slightly more progress the next day. Mom didn't plan on renting another hotel room that evening, but as we drove along the interstate passing Chattanooga, we got distracted by the *Rock City* sign painted on the side of an old barn. Another shelter claimed the visitors of *Rock City* could see seven states from Lookout Mountain.

A few minutes later, Danny spotted a third shed advertising that *millions* have seen *Rock City*. The fortress had a Fairyland Cavern. The temptation was too great, we felt Mom weakening. Sue pointed at the final ad touting a Mother Goose Village! Our own Mother Goose steered the car towards Lookout Mountain while we all sang *Chattanooga Choo Choo* and pulled imaginary train horns.

The natural attraction did not disappoint, but we were easily impressed, considering it was our first vacation since we were toddlers. Sue, Danny, and I were in awe as we took in the giant rock formations along the trail. We followed the path to a miniature golf course and then to a rock garden. At the end of the trail stood Lover's Leap.

We read the story carved on a plaque about a young Cherokee Indian who fell in love with a woman from a rival tribe. After he had been discovered, her family pushed him from the side of the ridge. Distraught from her loss, the young girl leaped to her own death. I reflected for a few moments before asking my mom if they were still down there. She suspected they were, but added that the animals probably had eaten them.

After another fast food meal and hotel stay, we leisurely checked out the next morning and headed south. Mom, determined to make the eight-hour drive to St. Petersburg, still agreed to stop for Stuckey's pecan logs at a roadside store.

We stocked up for the ride, and each enjoyed a fluffy, nougaty confection as we pulled out of the gravel driveway onto I-64 W. We almost made it to St. Pete by dinner time, but decided to make one final stop at the Georgia state line. The visitor center advertised freshly squeezed orange juice and a place to relax, which is exactly what we did.

We loved visiting our family in Florida. They all lived in bathing suits, had perpetual tans, and feet that were tougher than sand spurs. To us, stepping on the prickly burrs felt like walking on broken glass. The barnacles that grew on the seawalls were even more brutal. My intrepid cousins scaled the walls as if they were Spiderman. I whimpered as the jagged shells sliced through my skin, blood gushing from my heels.

Fascinated by my eldest cousin Bobby's ability to spear a stingray from the canoe, I became squeamish when it joined us for the ride home. Uncle Bob plopped the ray on their kitchen counter and cut the wings off with a sharp knife. He and Aunt Nancy used circular cutouts to create stingray "scallops" from the wings, which they sautéed for dinner. We dipped the delicious, little nuggets in melted butter and ate every morsel.

After dinner, Aunt Nancy had asked us to get rid of the stingray torso. Bobby tossed the carcass into the canal, directly between their home and Aunt Judi's house. One of the boys dared us to swim across the channel, warning that the bloody remains would attract sharks. Bobby added, "The kids from Florida would do it."

Peer pressure and our adventurous spirits emboldened us to jump off the seawall. We screamed and paddled across the canal as our hearts beat rapidly, expecting to lose a leg to a shark. The water was as black as the sky. I couldn't see anything in front of me and sweated as I swam. The short distance between my two aunt's homes seemed endless. We scrambled up the wall and stared at each other as we caught our breath, terror in all of our eyes.

Sue, Danny, and I survived another day to torture the visitors and employees of Cypress Gardens with our cousins. We lost Randy a few times at the theme park; although he was only six, no one seemed worried.

Our visit to Florida also introduced us to white sand beaches, the warm Gulf of Mexico, seagulls, fresh seafood, and grand hotels. To us, it was an oasis. We sadly headed for home with our souvenirs, as well as something we did not buy in a tourist shop.

Unbeknownst to any of us, we had picked up little critters in our hair from my cousins, who had just returned from a camping trip. The first week of school, we naively spread lice to most of the students at St. Barb's.

On the drive home from Florida, we groaned when we saw the Welcome to Ohio sign at the state border. Still ignorant of the bugs in our hair, our mom announced we were stopping at the Ohio State Fair.

To make extra money and earn free tickets, Dad worked security during the fairs each summer. We not only benefited from free admission as a perk of his job, but Dad was also able to secure seats along the catwalk so we could watch the bands.

In 1972, we saw The Osmonds in concert. The white-fringed jackets embellished in bling kept my attention the entire show. Well, that and Donny Osmond's smile and thick, dark hair. Despite Donny's charm, my family's most memorable concert was the previous summer when The Carpenters played their largest gig at the Ohio State Fair, attracting fifty-thousand attendees.

Dad spent the afternoon subduing unwieldy drunks while Mom secured front row catwalk seats for the rest of us. Sue, Danny, and I were along for the ride, but were pleasantly surprised by the talented siblings and enjoyed the soft rock songs.

Karen Carpenter spotted me standing on my seat, staring at her in awe as she strutted down the stage. She stopped and bent down, looked directly at me, and sang the remaining lyrics of *Close to You*. I stared back into her big, brown eyes and swayed to the music, engrossed in her sweet voice, her gentle spirit, and beautiful smile, reminding me of my mother.

Like the singer, Mom was a fragile person. She believed the world was full of good people, she smiled at strangers, and never took herself too seriously. Innocent and kind, Mom made everyone feel special. She showered the kids with endless compliments and made up songs about us that we'd sing in the car as we ventured out with Mother Goose on our next exciting activity. She was a rock star and idol to every kid in Kimmensville. Unfortunately, Mom would soon learn to live mostly with pain and sorrow.

The Teachers of St. Barb's

I passed the first-grade classroom on my way to the science lab and had a flashback of my most embarrassing day in elementary school. It was six years earlier, but I still recalled the traumatic afternoon. I blocked out her real name--it sounded like Mrs. Banana. I may not remember her given name, I will never forget her misguided anger towards my song. I was a first grader trying to fulfill my teacher's nutty obligation. I could have copped out like Melissa and sang *Twinkle, Twinkle Little Star*.

I wanted to sing something original to the class, so I ran next door to Aunt Judi's house for a suggestion. She always had creative ideas and loved music.

Judi was a child of the '60s, we thought of her as a cool hippy. She had long hair, wore bell-bottom jeans and crop tops, drove a red VW bug she named Crazy Alice after her mom, smoked Marlboro cigarettes, and pot. We found out about the pot as teenagers. It explained why she was always in a happy and mellow mood.

I ran up the shag stairs calling her name. The kids ran in and out each other's homes as if we owned them. At least that's what we regularly heard from the parents of Kimmensville. I found Aunt Judi washing Toodles in the bathtub and shared my school challenge with her.

She had the perfect song for me, *Little Buggie on the Wall*. It was surely an original sonnet. I quickly memorized the lyrics, and then ran home to find a cute outfit for my first classroom performance. I was nervous but confident. I memorized everything Aunt Judi suggested, including the little wiggles and curtsies.

Mrs. Banana's round, black-rimmed glasses sat on her oval face, framed by her pixie haircut. She resembled an owl in a dress. She looked in my direction and called my name. I proudly stood up, brushed the front of my skirt, walked to the head of the classroom, and launched into my song.

> Little Buggie on the Wall
> Don't you got no clothes at all
> Don't you got no pretty shirt?
> Don't you got no mini skirt?
> Little Buggie on the Wall
> Ain't you *cooooold?*

[Arms crisscrossed over my chest as I shivered]

[Curtsy to the classroom]

My teacher immediately rose from her wooden chair, walked swiftly across the classroom, and grabbed my elbow. The kids covered their mouths and giggled. She proceeded to drag me down the hallway to the principal's office as I asked her between sobs, *"What did I do wrong?"* She glared straight ahead with puckered lips, her patent leather shoes clicking loudly on the floor.

We sat in hard metal chairs as I was lectured on the appropriateness of my song and grammar. I argued that bugs don't wear clothes, so maybe they *were* cold. The principal proceeded to call my mother, who picked me up from school and drove me home.

Mom and I walked to Aunt Judi's house and shared the outcome of my performance. Judi felt terrible, but we all had a good laugh after reflecting on the naked bug song choice for such a rigid, pious establishment.

Mom also reminded us that Mrs. Banana used to be Sue's teacher. My parents were ecstatic when my big sister earned an A in Religion class. After scrutinizing her report card, they noticed black ink forming the letter F and a vertical pencil line completing the box-shaped A. Sue didn't realize she had to return the report card with a parent's signature. Their first

Parent/Teacher conference didn't go well. This instructor already had it in for us Gossage kids. Too bad she had left before Danny reached first grade, he would have reaped revenge for me.

That episode was my introduction to the Catholic school where I would study for eight tumultuous years. We didn't have to wear uniforms like most Catholic elementary schools. Our torture was attending church every day before school, waking up early so we could eat and still accept communion.

We slept in on Sundays, not allowing enough time for the required hour of fasting before the sacrament. Sue, Danny, and I made up for the missing meal by devouring donuts in the car on the way home. We wiped the evidence from our hands and faces, feigning hunger as we walked in the door and greeted our dad. That's when we'd consume our second luscious pastry of the day. I think this was Mom's way of bribing us to attend church each week. It seemed to work, not that we had much choice.

Not all of my elementary school teachers were a bad memory. One of the positive influences was the beautiful Miss Dietz. She was the crush of at least one male teacher, as well as my brother. Due to a teacher reassignment, Danny and I were lucky enough to have Miss Dietz as a teacher in second and six grades.

She wore her long, golden hair parted in the center, the trend in the early '70s. She was tall, thin, and wore pencil skirts, heels, and feminine blouses in soft colors. Her outfits were professional and stunning, considering the meager wage of a school teacher. Miss Dietz also made the curriculum interesting and engaged us in stories about her life, which made us feel even more connected to her.

My favorite teacher had a mad crush on Alan Alda. My dad watched his show, so I knew he starred in the TV program,

M*A*S*H. As I read through my monthly edition of *Tiger Beat* magazine looking for glossy photos of Andy Gibb, Peter Frampton, Leif Garrett, or Donny Osmond, I noticed a small side article about Alan Alda. It included his Fan Club information at the bottom. I was certain Miss Dietz would appreciate a shiny, autographed photo of his smiling face, as much as I would like one of my heartthrobs.

I immediately crafted a letter to the Alan Alda Fan Club. How could they turn me down when I told them about my beautiful, fair-haired teacher that talked about her dream to one day marry Mr. Alda.

Every afternoon, I ran to the mailbox at the end of our driveway, hoping for a response to my fan letter. A large manila envelope addressed to me, finally arrived. I carefully opened the package. It contained two shiny photographs and a letter from the *M*A*S*H* Fan Club.

The first image was a headshot of Alan Alda, his smile crooked but charismatic. In the bottom right corner, there was a dedication to Miss Dietz along with his autograph. The second shot was the full cast in front of a tent, the backdrop of the show in the opening credits. I could barely sleep that night. I was sure my teacher would be thrilled.

After she had finished laughing over my efforts on her behalf, she was delighted with the photos and my thoughtfulness. I stood there grinning as she thanked me and gave me a hug before she hung them on the corkboard in the front of the classroom, where they remained the rest of the year.

Alan Alda may have been her movie star infatuation, but we were pretty sure our PE teacher, Mr. Stanley, was a real-life crush. Our second-grade classroom had closet doors along one wall where the teachers stashed their supplies, and we stored our jackets and lunch boxes. The gym teacher must have arrived early that day to plot his practical joke on Miss Dietz. They did that to each other every once in a while.

Mr. Stanley was tall, dark-haired, tanned, and athletic with a bright smile that charmed just about every elementary school girl and probably their mothers, as well. The two of them looked like Barbie and Ken dolls. My friends and I all secretly hoped they would get married one day. Little girls are silly romantics that way.

When our teacher opened the closet doors to gather supplies for our first exercise of the day, six panicked chickens, wings madly flapping, burst out of the small space and ran through the aisles. The classroom went berserk, the kids running in circles, screaming louder than the fowl. Miss Dietz clearly had a poultry phobia, jumping up and down on tiptoe and screeching.

Mr. Stanley hid outside, finally exposing himself as the brains behind the mischievous plot. She sent us outside for a break as she scolded and laughed at Mr. Stanley, promising to reap revenge as he gathered up the chickens.

Our mother had told us Mr. Stanley and some friends bought a restaurant called the Red Dog Saloon. My sister and I both had a preteen obsession with dreamy Mr. Stanley, so we begged her to take us. Mom never wanted to deny her children anything in life and was always up for a fun time. She pulled out the phone book, checked the map in the back, and planned our adventure to East Sparta, Ohio. Of course, she let us bring a couple of friends along.

We primped and fussed with our hair until we were satisfied with our reflections in the floor length mirror. As we strutted to the car, my brother complimented us on our appearance. He was often the lone boy in a group of girls and never seemed to mind.

The Red Dog Saloon exceeded our expectations. We spotted the red structure, surrounded by a dirt parking lot filled with rusty Chevy and Ford pickup trucks. The white sign hung over a row of small windows lining the top floor. Mom parked her dark brown Ford sedan, and we crossed the lot, up the creaky stairs. Danny swaggered across the wooden porch and threw open the swinging saloon doors, Clint Eastwood-style.

Country music blared from speakers on the small stage as waitresses in tight shirts with cleavage swirled around the tables, balancing trays of drinks and plates of fried food. The impressive bar was lined with beautiful amber-colored bottles. We could see the reflection of the bar patrons through the wooden-framed mirror, "Red Dog Saloon" painted across the front. They were drinking and smoking as their heads bobbed to the music. The bartenders poured concoctions from colored bottles and served foamy draft beer.

We knew we didn't belong there, but we were with Mom and had come to visit our teacher. It all sounded so innocent when we planned the excursion; now we imagined the exciting stories we would tell our classmates on Monday.

The hostess greeted us, led us to a round table, and handed out greasy plastic menus with a bulldog cartoon on the front. My mom asked if Mr. Stanley was working, adding that we were his students. The pretty waitress smiled and promised to tell him we were here. We scanned the menu and decided on our typical meal of hamburgers and pop with a side of fries.

Anticipating Mr. Stanley's arrival, we were as excited as groupies at a concert. We finally spotted his wide shoulders and flowing, black hair. He was strutting our way, dressed in cowboy boots, jeans, and a white, button-down shirt tucked under a shiny belt buckle. Our teacher was no exception to the young men of the '70s who preferred long, feathered hair and tighter than average denim.

Mr. Stanley bent down and put his arms around the back of our shoulders, giving us all a friendly squeeze and big, pearly white smile. He laughed, saying how surprised and pleased he was to see some of his favorite students. As our curious mother often did with anyone that stopped long enough to ask the time, she quizzed our instructor about the bar and his involvement. When our food arrived, he went back to work, and we dreamily picked at our fries and nibbled at our burgers, taking in the sights and sounds of the saloon.

Mr. Stanley was the opposite of Miss Preece, my uptight, unmarried, fourth-grade teacher who didn't seem to like kids. If she knew about our visit to the tavern, she would have reprimanded my mother, as well as her peer.

My teacher wore layers of stockings and garments, all visible through her form-fitting, polyester dresses. The vibrant fabric, patterned with geometric shapes stretched across her round body. I vividly recall her navy blue, polyester dress with white circles the size of small plates, a thin belt cinched around her midsection separating her mounds like a snowman. Miss Preece's thick, round glasses and curly hair added to her circular ensemble. She bundled the curls on the top of her head, resembling a gigantic Shirley Temple.

Miss Preece had wanted to spend her remaining years teaching at a Catholic school in a small town. She joined St. Barb's in the late '70s, never anticipating the challenge my brother and his unruly friends would pose when they entered her class two years after me.

When she left the classroom, a few boisterous boys scooted their desks to the front, climbed on top, and jammed pencils into the holes of the fiber tiles. Everyone gave up their stash for this hoax. Miss Preece returned to the room, her eyes darting to the pencils jutting from the ceiling, erasers aimed for her head, ready to fall at any time. She balled up her fists, puckered her lips, spun on her heels, and stomped down the hall to the principal's office.

She could never prove my brother was guilty of most wrong doings in the room of docile-looking children, all sitting quietly crossing their hands on their desks. Every kid in the classroom would protect the delinquents, enjoying the torment they inflicted on this unpopular teacher. The administrators knew that Danny, Matt, and Shawn organized most gags in their classroom, but couldn't always prove it.

Danny was actually a good-natured boy, maintained perfect grades, excelled at sports, and charming young girls. He just liked to have a little fun at the expense of his least favorite faculty members.

Miss Preece finally caught Danny in action, passing a note to one of his cohorts in class. She unfolded the ruled sheet of paper to find a cartoon pencil sketch of herself, the rear-end filling the page. My brother's drawing skills were exceptional, both cartoon and realistic. He emphasized the imperfections and flaws of his subjects, this piece was no exception.

The caricature was clad in the familiar navy blue and white polka-dotted dress. He nailed every feature, from the tightly wound coils bunched on the top of her head to the chubby feet stuffed into her pointed heels. She froze, her hands shaking as she gripped the paper. Without speaking, the teacher once again headed directly for the principal's office.

Miss Preece retired from teaching that year. Principal Ferrell suggested my brother also consider his tenure at St. Barbara's, maybe a *public* junior high school would be a better fit.

Danny hung in there until seventh grade, then begged for a transfer to Tuslaw Intermediate for his last year of junior high school. His real motive was to avoid the teacher that intimidated him the most.

Danny met his rival when his seventh-grade class swapped rooms with the eighth graders, twice a day. Mrs.

Albright's claim to fame was teaching history and government to the upper classmates. She was not easily intimidated like Miss Preece or charmed like Miss Dietz. She was a strong force, not frightened by anyone.

Mrs. Albright was also a rather large woman, a dark bouffant sitting above her round face. Her makeup routine was remarkable, the liquid foundation was at least a shade or two darker than her skin and always ended abruptly at her jaw line. It looked as if she put a mask on her face every morning. I found it very distracting, but not as offensive as the Tabu perfume stench. She must have bathed in the spicy amber cologne every morning. If we couldn't smell her coming, we heard the swishing sounds of her pantyhose from her thighs rubbing together.

Mrs. Albright wasn't fond of a few kids at school. For various reasons, my brother and a kid in Sue's class were on the top of her Shit List. I'm not sure if her dislike of Bobby started before or after he stumbled down the aisle during morning Mass, reeking of booze and cigarettes.

Her brown face turned red, creating a burnt sienna tint, eyes blazing with anger. Bobby staggered, eventually collapsing on the red, velveteen carpet before he could reach the priest standing at the podium. Thank God. Mrs. Albright dragged him back down the aisle and through the swinging doors to the Cry Room. As she was scolding him, he threw up a bottle of vodka on her patent leather heels, earning him a two-week suspension.

Bobby won the last victory in the battle with Mrs. Albright. The students took offense to her afternoon habit of slowly pouring Coca-Cola into an ice-filled glass in front of us. On hot summer days, we watched as sweat dripped down our faces and we stuck to our fabricated wooden chairs, no air conditioning in the school house. Our teacher would savor the first sip, her eyes closed, always finishing with, "*Ahhhhhhhh.*" We licked our lips and ogled the drink. Students were not allowed to have drinks in the classrooms.

Our jealousy ended the day Bobby reaped revenge for all of us. When she left the room, he slipped a square of dark brown Ex-Lax in her pop. As the drink bubbled and fizzed, the kids began to panic. They held their breath, hoping she would be gone long enough to allow the Ex-Lax to dissolve.

Mrs. Albright returned just as the last bubble vanished. The class could barely contain themselves when she gulped her drink the rest of the period. I suspect she experienced some gentle overnight relief and assumed it was something she had eaten for lunch.

Mrs. Albright assigned an annual term paper to her seventh-grade students, introducing us to the hours of research and writing we could expect in high school, and hopefully college. When she approved Danny's topic for the project, John F. Kennedy, my brother grinned. The busy teacher forgot that I had chosen the same subject.

Danny ran home and begged me into recycling the research paper that earned me an A+. My hard work and many bike rides to the library paid off, dropping dimes to photocopy pages about the Bay of Pigs and Cuban Missile Crisis. It seemed a shame to let my report collect dust in a box. I relinquished the goods to Danny.

My little brother replicated my handwritten index cards, retyped my report verbatim, and copied my poster board – changing only the word I misspelled, "Assasination." Danny bound the plagiarized documents in a clear report cover and turned it in.

Later that day, he presented his topic in front of the classroom. Our overburdened teacher didn't recognize my work and awarded my brother a perfect grade for his account of our thirty-fifth president.

Our teachers had an impact on our young little psyches, both positive and frightening. The educators that made the biggest difference were those that freely gave their time, cared immensely, and motivated the indifferent. After eighth grade, I only saw a couple of my former teachers from St. Barb's. The ones that mattered the most were there when I needed them.

Misbehavin'

In the general vicinity of our homes, the Kimmensville gang had several locations to discover and explore. The forbidden barn remained one of our cherished hangouts.

Sue, Karlene, and I snuck up the grassy ramp to the massive entryway. Trying not to alert the parents with the loud screech, in unison, we slid the wooden doors across the tracks. It took a minute for our eyes to adjust to the darkness before we could safely cross the floor, avoiding the missing boards and a nasty tumble to the floor below.

The sun filtered through the rafters, shining rays of light across the old beams, making ghostly shadows of the abandoned tools. The smell was earthy, like compost, and the air was damp. Regardless of the temperature outside, entering the barn gave me a chill.

While we hunted materials for our latest invention, a squarish owl that lived in the beams scared us with his screech. He showed his displeasure by flexing his wings and spinning his head completely around. Like many kids in the 1970s, we had witnessed Linda Blair in *The Exorcist* mimic this demonic movement. We ran screaming through the apple orchard, only to return later.

The three of us carefully navigated the broken floor, keeping one eye on the owl. We came across an industrial-sized barrel in the far corner, covered in rust. I shook the drum, liquid swished at the bottom. Sue squeezed the black spigot mounted on the lid, freeing the foamy engine degreaser just as Sandy saw the barn door cracked open and joined us.

We abandoned our project and convinced her that the tub of pink foam was bubble gum shampoo. After she had fallen for our fib, we covered her silky, blonde tresses in the cleaner intended for machinery.

It did not work as well on hair as it did on a tractor engine. Sandy finally realized we were lying and ran home. We instantly regretted our behavior and wondered why we thought that was a good idea. Doris was rightfully upset with us. She spent the afternoon using every product she could locate to diminish the offensive diesel odor that penetrated her daughter's golden strands.

The adventures of our club were fun-filled, mischievous, and often dangerous. The tub of foam was not the only harmful substance that we found in the barn. While living in the farmhouse, Sue and I played a couple of "jokes" on our dear brother. I'm not sure where our mean streak came from, or if our behavior was due to sheer boredom and not thinking of the repercussions of our actions.

The worst and almost fatal prank we pulled was draining oil from a corroded tractor and persuading Danny it was root beer. After a big gulp, he ran into the house screaming, oil dripping from his chin. Dad rushed him to the Massillon ER to have his stomach pumped.

For our hurtful behavior, Sue and I received a thorough tongue lashing and spanking from our mother. Danny returned home that evening with an ice cream cone in hand and a disappointing glare for his sisters; both were justified.

The second horrible trick we played on naïve, little Danny was convincing him that his spongy, blue Nerf ball was edible. After the tractor oil incident, he should not have believed anything his sisters told him. But, we compared it to the blue cotton candy we ate at the fair. He finally took a bite and swallowed enough to warrant another trip to the hospital. The nurses placed the familiar tube down his throat to expel the polyester resin.

As karma would have it, I had plenty of turns on a gurney, under bright lights in the emergency room to suture wounds, set broken bones, and apply casts. The difference being, all of my injuries were my own fault.

I caught my left ear on a nail when I neglected to see the missing step and fell through the attic stairs. I can't explain how I broke my thumb during fifth-grade gym class or how I tore my knee open on a nail, minutes before our family portrait appointment at Olen Mills. I even ended up in a full arm cast for eight weeks after falling from my bike while delivering Girl Scout cookies. I definitely wasn't a graceful child.

Sue only experienced the trauma of the emergency room a few times. Her most severe injury was losing a chunk of flesh from her forehead while trying to break up a dogfight to save our pet, Sergeant. She avoided a second trip because of her bad aim. She was five when she found my dad's handgun and almost shot off her big toe.

Our emergency room visits started the day Sue and I woke up early and settled on the couch at the farmhouse to watch Saturday morning cartoons. We were still wearing our long, silky gowns with ruffles around the sleeves, her straight hair smashed and mine frizzy.

After eating a bowl of Fruit Loops, we remembered to take the Fred Flintstone vitamins Mom always placed next to our breakfast. They made us healthy, so after chewing the character of our choice, a purple Barney for me and pink Pebbles for Sue, we justified another few vitamins. As we watched *Bugs Bunny*, we counted the pills on the smooth fabric of our nightgowns that stretched across our laps, both of us double checking to make sure the piles were even. We consumed the delicious chewables as if they were M&Ms until the bottle was empty.

My parents eventually stumbled downstairs to start their day and noticed the empty bottle of vitamins sitting next to their sleepy girls, still fixated on the antics of the silly wabbit. We didn't understand why Mom and Dad were so worried. They woke Danny up, threw us in the back of the car, and sped to the hospital for our own unpleasant gastric lavage.

The unsympathetic nurse put us in the same room. We not only experienced what we put our little brother through, twice, but we also had to watch each other being tormented by the clear rubber tube. The nurses repeatedly thrust them down our throats until we felt like empty sacks.

One cloudy afternoon, my mom dropped us off at the Weslin Theater for a matinee. We groaned when we noticed the grumpy manager was taking tickets. We questioned his career choice because he did not like children. After buying our tickets at the box office, we waited in line to hand our ticket stub to the little man. Outside of his earshot, we wondered why his fingers were so short and stubby. They looked chopped in half but had fingernails. This, of course, gave Danny and Jimmy an idea.

As the crowd slowly streamed into the theater, Danny and Jimmy bent their fingers in half and wedged their tickets between the first two nubs. We approached the manager, properly dressed in his three-piece suit and tie. Stifling their laughs, the boys handed him the stub between their folded fingers. The angry man turned red, snatched the tickets from them, and grumbled obscenities that were not under his breath.

We giggled as we all piled into the snack bar area, slapping Danny and Jimmy on the back. After we had stocked up on movie treats, we found a row of empty seats a few rows from the screen, just the way we liked it.

Sandy was a few years older than the rest of us, and we all looked up to our big friend. Dena was enamored with our neighbor and wanted to sit next to her. I was already seated next to Sandy.

When the cartoons ended, I jumped up to refill my pop before the start of the main attraction. The lights were out when I returned, the movie reel was displaying the countdown. I squinted in the dark, walking slowly until I located the back of my brother's head and knew I had reached our row.

Shuffling sideways to my seat, I noticed Dena was in my spot. I quietly asked her to move, she refused. She said it was her seat now, "Move your meat, lose your seat." Her original chair was at the end of our group, next to strangers. I angrily whispered, *"Get out of my seat, now!!"* Dena refused to move and followed up her rebuttal by throwing her tub of popcorn in my face. My instincts immediately kicked in, and I dumped my freshly filled, ice-cold pop over her head. That got the shrieking Dena to jump out of my seat.

I didn't think the pop incident through. After that move, I wasn't able to enjoy the show. The manager was angrier than we'd ever seen him. His little legs stomped down the aisle until he reached our row. He pointed a nubby finger at Dena and me and told us to follow him to his office, *immediately*!

We bowed our heads and endured the walk of shame up the carpeted aisle-way and through the double doors. Moviegoers were forbidden to climb the staircase leading to the second floor, so I thought this part of the punishment was actually kind of neat.

Dena and I sat in his office in overstuffed chairs opposite his wooden desk and watched the cars driving down Lincoln Way. He demanded our phone numbers, then dialed the rotary phone with his stubby finger. We sneered at each other, refusing to apologize.

After escorting us out of the building into the custody of my mom, the manager slammed the doors behind him. We complained that our little quarrel did not warrant being kicked out. Sue and Danny told me later I didn't miss anything, the

76

show wasn't that great. I'm not sure if they were telling the truth or trying to make me feel better, but it worked.

Our adventures with Dena were short but memorable. Judi and John decided to move to a warmer climate and chose Florida as their destination. They built a house across the canal from Aunt Nancy in St. Petersburg so she could continue to grow up with her cousins.

My mom's weakest parenting skill was discipline; it was also her least practiced trait. Any rules she did try to enforce, were mostly ignored, so she invented the Big Bopper.

Mom had the tolerance to put up with many kids at a time and rarely lost her temper. The few times she did get mad, she paddled us with a wooden pizza board that she ordered from a school fundraising catalog specifically for this purpose.

When the paddle had arrived along with wrapping paper and flavored popcorn, she immediately penned **BIG BOPPER** in permanent marker down the handle. When Mom headed to the hall closet in anger, we knew to run to the golf course and scatter three different ways. Whoever she caught got it for the other two, it all worked out, we took turns.

Her spankings never hurt us, but we writhed in pain so she would stop. Afterward, the three of us would huddle in one of our bedrooms and laugh. Mom eventually caught onto our acts, and the Big Bopper landed a little harder on our derrieres.

Danny thought he was clever the time he knew a paddling was in his future and put on eight pairs of underwear, then squeezed into his blue jeans. My brother was busted when Mom noticed his pants were unusually snug, and he had trouble walking. She made him peel off the extra undies, and because Danny tried to fool her, she threw in a few more whacks.

My worst whooping was a misunderstanding. Dad had bought a new 35 mm camera and was snapping pictures of us all day. He opened the unlocked bathroom door and took a shot of my unsuspecting Mom sitting on the toilet, intending to throw the print away.

A week later, Mom picked up the pictures from the Fotomat, threw them on the kitchen table, and reminded my dad to toss the one of her on the commode. I snuck it into my school folder.

My friend Lisa Ruegg lived on a dairy farm, and we spent many weekends having sleepovers at each other's homes. Lisa was keenly aware of how much time my mom spent secluded in our bathroom, mostly for peace and solitude from her boisterous family. If Mom was indisposed and we needed to ask her something, we walked in, sat on the carpeted floor, and made our request. I thought my friend would find the picture amusing.

After school, Lisa and I huddled in the back row of the bus and watched the funniest person we knew walk up and down the aisle as she performed her stand-up comedy shtick. Donna's imitation of Roseanne Roseannadanna from *Saturday Night Live* was always on point. "*Last Thursday*, I quit *smoking*! Now, I'm *depressed*, I've *gained weight*, my *face* broke out, I'm *nauseous*, I'm *constipated…*" Until Pete yelled at her to sit down, Donna was responsible for the entire busload of kids roaring with laughter.

As we drove down Kenyon, I snuck the picture from my folder and let Lisa take a peek. We both covered our mouths and quietly giggled at the crude photo.

That afternoon, Mom happened to meet us at the end of the road to walk us home. My siblings told her that I showed the picture of her indisposed to my *entire* classroom. She was furious. I argued that it wasn't true, "I only showed…" Mom grabbed my arm before I could finish. She was so mad about the accusation she wasn't listening to my side of the story.

I wriggled out of her grasp and ran down the street, veering right onto the golf course. I wasn't sure of my plan until the apple orchard came into view. I ran for the tallest tree I knew I could climb. Before anyone saw me, I clambered up the trunk and hid behind the leaves. For hours, I watched my family and friends spread out across the golf course, screaming my name, over and over.

They eventually gave up and went inside. I stayed in my hideout until sunset, which ended up being a bad idea. When I walked in the back door, still carrying my school books, Mom was not only angry, she was worried. That evening, my rendezvous with the Big Bopper was inevitable.

Sometimes Mom knew we were misbehaving and chose to look the other way, other times she was completely unaware of our mischief. A dangerous but fun idea struck us during an annual dentist appointment at Dr. Shaw's in downtown Massillon.

Dr. Shaw sported worse teeth than any of his patients, which was obviously an unfavorable advertisement for his business. I spent my visits staring at the crooked teeth poking out of his gums in the most precarious way, wondering why he didn't take care of that dental mess.

Every year, Mom made four adjoining appointments in one afternoon. After we had grown bored with the *Highlights* magazines, we were allowed to explore one of the tallest buildings in Massillon. Towering at six floors, plus a mezzanine, we had plenty to keep us distracted.

The elevators were so old they needed an attendant to operate them, who ironically looked exactly like the decrepit, silent men in drab suits that worked the lifts in old, scary movies. We knew the grumpy man despised us. We didn't care.

While Mom was in the dental chair, we rode from floor to floor, ran up and down the staircase, summoning the elevator to take us to yet another random level. The operator eventually kicked us out and refused to play our little game, so we decided to check out the restroom on the top floor.

The open windows overlooking the traffic on Erie Street conveniently did not have screens. Sue, Danny, and I all grabbed rolls of toilet paper and carefully unraveled a few feet. Aiming for the sidewalk on the opposite side of the street, we securely held the ends and hurled the rolls from the windows. The toilet paper streams were beautiful, like a white rainbow. When we told the neighborhood kids about our afternoon, they were upset they weren't there.

The Kimmensville kids spent so much time together we started to feel like we were all siblings. We claimed that the teasing and punching were all in good fun, but it caused a bucket full of tears and several injuries over the years. The latest victim usually plotted their revenge over several days and had to be creative about surprising the other kid. In the end, the score was fairly even, with Jimmy slightly down because of the Dog Poop Incident, as it became known in my household.

I didn't witness the grizzly scene, so I can't be sure if Jimmy instigated the older girls to cause such torment, or they were just bored and feeling annoyed at their sidekick that day.

Jimmy was exceptional at teasing us. When he flung insults our way, we chased and punched him until he cried and ran home. About an hour later, he returned, and we acted as if nothing happened. After drying our eyes and swallowing our pride, we all crawled back to our clan because we were family.

The doorbell chimed, I heard my mom greet Harriett at the front door in her typical welcoming style. Jimmy's mom did not reciprocate. Instead, I heard her crossly explain to my mom that *she* would be washing Jimmy's play clothes. She threw them on the porch and walked up Kimmens to the old farmhouse. The clothes were covered in dog shit.

Sue and Karlene confessed to rolling Jimmy back and forth like a rolling pin, holding his arms and legs so he couldn't escape until his clothes were covered in the putrid excrement. After telling Sue she was grounded for the week, Mom made her rinse them outside using the garden hose before she allowed her to use our washing machine. The fact Harriett knocked on our door and not Bev's, made me think Sue was the ring leader in that persecution.

One dull afternoon, Danny and Jimmy led their own poo assault. Plenty of neighbors were equestrians, so there was never a shortage of road apples lying around. When riding our bikes, we had to be keenly aware of the warm piles. The horse poo came to mind when Danny and Jimmy were scheming about how to irritate an annoying neighbor on Kenyon.

They filled a paper bag with manure and swiped a lighter from Jimmy's mom. After burning the bag of dung, they pressed the doorbell and hid in the brush across the street from the old grump's house. The target of their ruse did precisely as planned. He flung open the door, stomped on the blazing bag to extinguish the flames, and was met with a warm, soft squish under his slippers.

Things got a little rough in Kimmensville at times, and quite a few punches were thrown; a couple of them landed squarely on my face. Sandy and I were in an argument about something stupid, and it carried over to the next day. While I was making breakfast, the screen door opened and Sandy stomped into our kitchen. We continued our silly argument before she took a few steps toward me, punched me in the left eye, turned on her heels, and ran through the front yards until she reached her home. I was too stunned to chase her or do much of anything except grab an ice pack and lie on the couch. It did hurt for a couple of days, but I felt sort of tough sporting my first official black eye.

The second time I was punched in the face was also a surprise. Pete pulled the yellow bus to a halt as the red lights blinked and the stop sign jutted from the left side. I was wedged in the line of sleepy school kids, all standing in front of Mr. Reed's house. Completely unprovoked, a neighbor kid named Brad spun around and belted me in the nose. I saw his fist coming at me, I couldn't react in time. Stunned from the impact, I stumbled back a few steps, the kids behind me catching my fall.

With no hesitation, I swung my right leg back as far as I could and kicked Brad squarely between the legs, dropping him to the ground. Pete hobbled down the stairs of the bus with his bum leg and demanded that we cease the battle. That was not a problem. Within a minute, we had managed to incapacitate each other.

Brad and his friends had an ongoing quarrel with the Kimmensville Club. I assumed slamming my nose was payback from a previous scuffle. Though, I did not deserve the retribution since they started the BB gun war.

We meandered down Highlander Avenue, our regular route to buy junk food at John George's. Suddenly, three boys jumped from behind a tree and began firing at us with BB guns. I was happy to be wearing my shiny, letterman-style jacket to shield myself from the pellets. I heard the others scream when they felt the sting of the tiny bullets on their skin. That afternoon, we returned wearing jackets and armed with our own BB guns, surprising the boys of Highlander Avenue.

I was in fifth grade when I had my last fight with Brad. The bus dropped us at the usual spot, in front of Mr. and Mrs. Jones' house on the corner of Kimmens and Kenyon. As we passed by, I usually admired the impeccable landscaping and lawn ornaments scattered about the lot. This particular day, I wasn't paying attention to the yard, so I didn't see Brad and his friend Scott pop out from behind one of her pine trees.

It was too late to outrun them, so I tried to fend them off. I quickly realized I didn't have the strength to fight two preteen boys. I ended up on the grass, flat on my back. Scott held me down while Brad punched me. Until my siblings pulled them off of me, I fought back and shielded my face with my arms. I stumbled home, defeated.

Mom was furious when she saw the shape I was in. She called their parents, demanding an end to the Hatfield and McCoy feud boiling between their children. The parents agreed to a truce, and the boys were punished for beating me up. They were livid, but when I saw them around the neighborhood and stuck my tongue out, our treaty prevented them from doing anything about it.

I also had an adversary in elementary school. Steven was a thin kid with long, skeletal legs, a fair complexion, and a close-shaved haircut. He cackled like Jack Skellington from *Nightmare Before Christmas* and sort of resembled him. Steven's favorite past time seemed to be teasing other kids.

He called out the chubby kids and those with glasses. Our slight bully was far from perfect, but pointed out the faults of others and then giggled while he waited for their reaction. When it came to teasing me, he was a glutton for punishment.

Because of my propensity to stand up to the bully and represent the passive kids, I was nicknamed Bulldog by my Catholic school teachers. My stature may have also had something to do with the label. I was in eighth grade before I started growing vertically until then my expansion was mostly around the middle.

Steven was unrelenting and kept coming back for more pain and humiliation. I would shove or kick him for each mean barb he delivered, yet he continued his insults. Until the day

Steven started bringing me gifts on the bus. I never saw them as payoffs, I just thought he liked giving me things.

It started innocently with pencils. Our teachers made us write until we had calluses on our knuckles, I could always use a few extra #2s. One afternoon, Steven gave me a gold-plated, scalloped necklace that eventually turned green. I wasn't much of a jewelry girl anyway. The big score was the day he gifted me his pocket knife. My brother had one, so I was excited to compare blades with Danny when I got home. I kept all of this from my parents, I saw no reason to tell them about such petty trinkets.

I eventually realized he was trying to bribe me so I would let him get away with his behavior. No chance. I continued to stick up for myself and my friends, but the gifts were lovely. It all ended the day he gave me his plastic piggy bank, half filled with coins.

I lugged it home on the bus, down Kimmens from our bus stop, and straight to my bedroom. Sue immediately told Mom that I had some kid's piggy bank and she confronted me with questions about my loot. I didn't ask for it, I argued, he just *gave* it to me. Mom explained that was very generous of him, but I could not accept it. I was confused because we wrote thank you notes when someone gave us a gift, whether we liked it or not, and never gave it back. I finally relented and returned Steven's life savings to him the next day, politely declining his gift.

Not long after this incident, he moved to Texas with his family. My cause for protecting the school kids became non-existent, as did my presents.

Everybody Loves a Parade...and a Few Cheers

The Kimmensville Club didn't always terrorize each other and the people who brought us into this world. Sandy's dad was crazy about the kids in the neighborhood. Ronnie was our go-to guy when we wanted a ride to John George's for pop and potato chips, a thick crust pizza from Kraus', pocket change, or just a good laugh. His facial expressions had a Jerry Lewis-like quality, and he had a wicked sense of humor. Sandy's dad could make his eyes bulge out when he wanted to scare us, and it worked.

Ronnie taught us how to burp vociferously on demand. I was his best student. Practicing next to our open kitchen window, I burped so loudly that a golfer stopped in mid-swing and looked around. He most likely expected to see a bullfrog that wandered too far from the pond.

We knew we pushed the limits with our requests of Ronnie and didn't want to burn him out, so we invented cheers to earn our rewards. Most of our clan was girls, the boys were used to us running the show. Their muscles and laid-back temperaments were exactly what we needed to support our pyramid.

Our classic pizza cheer was incredibly uncreative. We must have been hungry the day we came up with, "*P - I - Z - Z - A. Pizza! Pizza! Yay yay yay!*" We chanted the lyrics to Ronnie as we formed a shaky pyramid, Sandy posing on top and Sue doing a split in the front.

One particular shout-out made Mr. and Mrs. Lowers turn red, but our efforts did earn us a treat. It was also the one cheer Danny and Jimmy refused to perform for any amount of cheesy goodness. Mainly because we insisted they shake their hips from side to side after each verse. It went something like this:

85

I'm a *mmm* lemon baby
I'm a *mmm* sack of 'taters
I'm the *mmm* hottest baby in town!

[Extra hip checks]

When it *mmm* comes to lovin'
I'm the *mmm* hottest oven
I'm the *mmm* hottest baby in town!

[Arms swinging wildly in the air, emphasizing the final hip shake]

Mom took us to a few parades in downtown Massillon where marching bands and floats sailed past as we waved back like beauty queens. The people lucky enough to hitch a ride on a float tossed gum and candy that we scrambled for alongside the other kids. The parades gave us the idea to form our own processions down Kimmens Road.

We mimicked the parade outfits using bygone costumes and accessories discovered in our toy boxes. My cousin's house was where we started our scavenger hunt for articles of clothing.

Leanne volunteered to sew outfits for our school plays, Halloween, and when she had extra fabric. We fought over the two shiny, gold capes she created when she found herself with a few spare yards of crinkled lamè. She weaved thick red yarn into the neckline so we could secure the glittery cloaks around our necks. We agreed it was Danny and Jimmy's turn to wear them since the girls usually put first dibs on the costumes.

They also liked to wear the capes while zipping along the golf course on our mini bikes, like superheroes on a mission. The fabric flapped in the wind, the tires left muddy tracks in their wake that Weany would certainly notice.

In addition to the gold lamè cape, Danny wore a curly, brown wig Mom donned in the '70s, round sunglasses, a tank top, and red shorts. He laced up his roller skates and gripped a set of bronze cymbals to complete his look. Liberace would have been proud.

The parade began at Sandy's house, each of us dressed in our garb with an instrument in hand to draw attention as we traipsed down the street. Sandy wore her majorette outfit and twirled a baton, lifting her knees high in the air, leading the pack down Kimmens. Colleen pulled a Red Flyer wagon carrying random neighbor pets also outfitted for the occasion. Banging and yelling, we passed by the parents standing at the end of the driveways.

We had to find other ways to entertain the neighborhood because our families were getting tired of interrupting their chores to humor us. During our next clubhouse meeting, Sandy had a terrific suggestion. It was a creative outlet for us, we were sure the adults would enjoy it, and we could make money.

That weekend, Ronnie and Doris had planned to host a party for the Kimmensville parents, as well as a few other friends. We began our preparations for the big debut immediately. This could be a huge win for the clubhouse slush fund.

The support beams in Sandy's basement proved to be ideal end posts for our stage curtain. Danny and Karlene tied a clothesline to two poles and tossed bed sheets across the taut latex rope. Sandy and I followed them with wooden clothes pins, securing the linens. Facing the stage, Jimmy lined up folding chairs for our audience members. Doris' laundry room was being transformed into the dressing room.

St. Valentine's Day was nearing so the first skit would feature Sue as *The Valentine Lady*. She changed into a pink tutu, wedged a plastic tiara in her hair, squeezed ballet slippers on her feet, and wrapped the ribbon around her ankles, leaving a few inches to tie a bow. We all sat in a circle on the basement floor, planning Sue's song and dance routine as we tore sheets of pink construction paper into confetti sized pieces. Colleen supplied the beautiful velvet purse with drawstrings that would hold the shredded paper, topping off Sue's outfit.

Danny was assigned the duty of ushering the patrons to their seats, and eventually becoming the stagehand when the production began. Jimmy collected money in a tin coffee can from the unsuspecting parents lined up at the door, digging in their pockets for a donation. My little brother escorted each parent to a folding chair lined up in front of our makeshift curtains.

Karlene was assisting the star of the first act, securing her headdress and calming her nerves. After everyone had been seated comfortably, our stagehand released the clothes pins to reveal a sea of pink and white crepe paper streaming from the metal pipes overhead.

A quiet order from the director marked the start of our performance. The Valentine Lady appeared stage left. Sue pranced around the basement floor in her pink bodice, the scratchy tulle bouncing in unison to her pointed steps. She grabbed handfuls of confetti from the velvet purse, waved her arm dramatically in the air, sprinkling the pieces we'd have to painstakingly pick up later. Sue danced atop the colorful scraps as she sang the lame song we wrote:

I am the Valentine *La-DY*
La-DY
La-DY
I am the Valentine *La-DY*
La-DY
And I'm here to bring you cheer

[*Repeat until confetti is gone*]

The audience cringed, secretly hoping we would focus our creative talents somewhere other than the recording business. We subjected our forced participants to a few more skits, including a scene from the sitcom *All in the Family* where Karlene played the conservative, blue-collar Archie Bunker. She sat in Ronnie's old recliner and threw out bigoted barbs and insults to Edith and son-in-law, Meathead, portrayed by Sandy and Jimmy, respectively.

My preferred act to pull off was a lip sync rendition of *Barracuda* by Heart, along with my backup singers. As the song blared from Sandy's record player balancing on the washing machine, I tossed my big, curly hair, strutted across the stage, and played air guitar.

Imitating Ann Wilson in her glory days, we bent our knees, sinking to the floor as we sang the angry lyrics, *"Down, down, down, down on my knees."* We jumped in the air as we screamed, *"Ooh, Barracuda!"*

By the time our show ended, the room was howling with laughter. The entire cast took the final bow, enjoying the praise and energy of the audience, thinking about how we would spend the change in the coffee can.

Our shows continued, and we were itching for a Mr. Microphone. My mom finally bought us the knock-off version from Sears. We tried it in our plays, but the metal transmitter shocked our lips when we got too close, so no one wanted to use it while performing.

Instead, we imitated the famous Mr. Microphone commercial with a handsome, blonde guy in a convertible. He used the microphone to transmit his pickup line through the car radio as they drove past a teenage girl. The young lady next to him in the car sneered and shoved her flirtatious boyfriend.

We talked Mom into slowly driving the car up and down Kimmens a few times so we could reenact the commercial. A few kids stood on the side of the road, acting cool and flipping their hair while the rest of us piled into the car. Mom slowly drove past them as we hung out the window gripping the microphone and repeating the famous line, "Hey, good lookin'! We'll be back to pick you up later!"

At a clubhouse meeting one morning, our entrepreneurial spirit was in full swing. We discussed a new angle to earn money that did not involve charging our parents for amusing them.

Mom was planning a trip to Bordner's Grocery store later that afternoon, which meant we could ride along and when she wasn't looking, throw a few things in the cart. We hid the lemonade mix under the groceries and left the store to wander up and down the aisles of the five-and-dime next door.

We all had enough change in our pockets for a few sweets that we carefully selected from the piles of candy separated by small glass panes. This was the same candy store Sue stole from when she was five years old.

Mom had found the confiscated items in her shorts when Sue changed and neglected to hide her stolen goods. My older sister was driven back to the store, marched up to the counter, made to apologize, and admit she took the candy without paying. That humiliating story was enough to convince Danny and me to pay for our goods, at least for a few more years.

Our new venture was an honest business, but it did require pilfering supplies and snacks from our parents. Danny snuck the sweet lemonade mix out of a grocery bag when we got home, stuffed it under his shirt, and casually walked out the back door.

Our friends combed their kitchens for Tupperware pitchers and paper cups. Colleen brought a package of cookies, and Sandy grabbed a cash box for the money we would hopefully earn. Tommy had a poster board leftover from a school project that we used to make our sign.

Danny and Colleen, our local artists, designed the advertising material. The creative pair drew a glass of cold lemonade, sweat dripping from the side, and bumble bees swirling around the sugary drink. The bulbous letters stated our purpose, "Lemonade for Sale - 25¢ / Glass."

Sandy helped Karlene drag a folding table from her garage, and the boys hauled a couple of chairs from Jimmy's, we set up shop near the twenty-fourth green. Sue secured our sign to the table using the masking tape she borrowed from my dad's workbench.

We picked a shady spot near the shrubs that separated the putting green from the tee, a remote corner far from the clubhouse bar. Rarely did a golfer deny our smiles and pitches for "*Lemonade! Ice cold lemonade!! Get your lemonade right here!!*" We were only berated once for our catchy spiel when the younger kids prematurely chanted our pitch and caused a man to miss his putt.

After giving us a dollar and only ordering one or two drinks, the golfers often told us to keep the change. We were always very thankful since we had to split our meager proceeds by eight. Our financial hopes ran high when a trio of players asked us if we had any beer to sell them, they said they'd pay a buck a can.

Our eyes lit up at the thought of the quick cash, we looked at each other and shrugged our shoulders. No harm checking to see if Dad had any cold brews in the fridge. I darted up the hill and ran through our back door, confronting my mom in the kitchen. I casually asked if I could snag a couple of Dad's beer cans to sell to some thirsty golfers. She refused my appeal, afraid he would notice if they were missing. I returned with a frown and delivered the bad news.

The afternoon sun started to set in the big Ohio sky, so we shut down our shop and split the money evenly between the gang. There was still time to ride our bikes to John George's and spend the cash now burning a hole in our pockets. Patience was not our strongest virtue.

Danny had a chopper bike with a banana seat and high sissy bar, allowing enough room for Tommy. The group rode east on Kimmens and picked up speed when we coasted down Highlander Avenue to the corner store. We hung out on the concrete porch, lapping our ice cream, and reminiscing about our successful lemonade stand, already planning the next one.

It was starting to get dark, so we rode home and waved goodbye as we turned into our driveways. Danny yelled, "*See ya' later alligator!*" Everyone screamed back, "*After a while crocodile!*"

The Nun and the Frog

The biology assignment from Sister Lucille challenged us to bring the most enormous and gruesome victim for her next science experiment. I had the perfect plan, but it was not a task I was willing to do on my own.

I solicited the assistance of my brother and Jimmy. I knew if I actually pulled this off, she would be thrilled. I was afraid of this particular nun and learned at the start of the year, it was best to please the sister rather than cross her.

Sister Lucille was not your typical Catholic cleric. She wore polyester skirts in various shades of blue donned by oversized, cotton, short-sleeve blouses with blue flowers. Even her orthopedics, necessary to support her thick thighs and cankles, were navy. Her arms were the shade of bacon fat with hairy moles scattered along the surface. She was an intimidating woman with broad shoulders and frizzy, gray hair, exemplifying the terrible hair products available in the '80s. Because of her wardrobe and the fact she was perpetually angry, my brother nicknamed her The Blue Bitch.

The Blue Bitch routinely lost her temper, spit flying from her overlapping, coffee stained teeth, her cheeks as red as the carpet in church. When we misbehaved, she was the only female teacher that offered an option between a whack with a two-by-four or detention.

The paddling was the best choice, but also the most painful. Detention involved notifying our parents we would miss the bus ride home because of our misconduct, which often included a second punishment. It was best to bend over, take a deep breath, and hope you could withstand the wallop headed towards your backend. She appeared to take pleasure in whacking the boys, not the most serene vestal.

My seventh-grade year, I sat near the row of windows that jutted out like awnings when they were propped open, shading the grass outside. Anyone seated near the windows during a tornado drill had a critical task. Opening the windows would relieve the pressure and save the school from destruction, or so we were told. We also put textbooks on our heads and hid under our desks, believing this would save us from a violent storm ripping through the city.

It was a muggy afternoon in the old, two-story, brick schoolhouse. We were all fidgeting, anxiously awaiting the bell, including Sister Lucille. She asked Mike to stand and read out of his textbook. I don't recall exactly how their argument started, but he gave her an attitude.

Sister Lucille raged, her eyes bulged, and the familiar spit flew from her lips. She confronted him, her poufy hair standing a bit higher, pointing her finger in his face. He stood his ground, looked her directly in the eyes, and said with contempt, *"You Bitch!"*

Our southpaw sister swung her left arm back and slapped him across the face. The *smack* echoed through the classroom, his right cheek red from the impact. Mike was a tall, lean kid from the track team who lived in the neighborhood behind the school. It only took a few seconds for him to make his move.

He quickly swerved past her stocky frame, bolted down the aisle, out the door, and down the school hallway towards the exit. The classroom full of students sat frozen and wide-eyed, listening to the patter of his shoes on the linoleum floor as he headed down the hall.

Sister Lucille pursued her scapegoat in her clunky, rubber-soled footwear. Every student in the classroom jumped out of their seats and crowded around the windows, craning our necks out of the openings to see the drama unfold. Before we lost sight of him, Mike passed the school gym and cleared the turn on Twenty-Eighth Street.

We quickly returned to our seats, flipped open a book, and pretended to read quietly. Sister Lucille burst into the classroom, panting, and sweating from the chase. As she crossed the front of the room, she waved her hands wildly in the air motioning for us to stand up.

We stood like shaking hostages, terrified to do anything except follow her commands. She ordered us to *"Pray that the devil leaves the room!!"* She acted as if evicting a demon had been covered in religion class. How does a classroom full of preteens react to a fanatical nun dictating that we conduct an exorcism in the middle of our English lesson? We carefully snuck glances at each other and with bewilderment, repeated her wild prayers.

Surprisingly, Sister Lucille survived her ordeal as an educator. It was 1980 and adults could still smack kids without getting slapped back with a lawsuit. Her reign of torture at St. Barb's continued, this time it was directed at innocent amphibians.

Seventh-grade science class was held at the south corner of the brick building, past the first-grade classroom. We knew Sister Lucille would be waiting for us in the lab like Dr. Frankenstein, hovering over the beakers and microscopes.

My classmates and I sauntered down the corridor with no urgency, our footsteps echoing off the eggshell-colored walls. Crown molding ran horizontally down the hallway, accenting the dome ceilings. We passed the other classrooms, brown wooden doors propped open exposing the small window panes that ran the length of the wall. They formed a grid pattern, overlooking the grassy lawn and the church next door. I would have taken a detour had I been aware of the barbaric assignment awaiting us.

That afternoon at the bus stop, I ran after Danny and Jimmy to enlist their aid for my homework obligation. To meet Sister Lucille's expectations, I needed the assistance from a couple of country boys. They were up for it, but Jimmy made us promise we wouldn't tell his mom.

We weren't sure if Harriet would have approved of our plan. Our mom ignored or agreed to everything we could dream of. We knew she would not be a problem. Jimmy's primary concern was his curfew since our prey rarely appeared before sunset. The pond was less than half a mile from Jimmy's house, but not all of the parents permitted their kids to run around on the golf course after dark.

Danny grabbed a towel from the bathroom while I searched for a bucket and golf clubs in the garage. I thought irons would work best. Dad's workbench was a haven for kids on an adventure. He hated it when we touched his stuff, meaning anything he owned, we did it all the time.

My brother and I walked to the end of the driveway and filled the bottom of the bucket with stones we found on the edge of the unpaved street. The rocks were heavy enough to knock a bullfrog out, hopefully not kill it. The real torture would be delayed until the next day, in our seventh-grade lab at the hands of our Kevorkian nun.

As planned, Jimmy successfully eluded his parents as they settled in for an after-dinner libation. Bucket and weapons in hand, Danny, Jimmy, and I met in the apple orchard at dusk. We trekked across the golf course to the pond near the twenty-second green. The glow of the moonlight reflecting on the still water was ideal for our intentions that evening but also created a ghostly effect.

We listened to nature's orchestra, the chorus of deep roars from the bullfrogs and the noisy crickets hiding in the grass. Gently placing our equipment on the lawn, we spoke in hushed tones, trying not to scare them off. The shaft of light allowed us to spot their heads and bulging eyes poking out of the water between the reeds. We each grabbed a few rocks and slowly crept up on the oblivious creatures.

Using the rock skipping skills our dads taught us, we each chose unwilling victims and aimed our stones at the top of their heads. In a stern but soft tone, I instructed the boys to just hit them hard enough to knock them out. I thought it was worth reminding them this was not a kill mission, more of a frog-napping.

We quietly crept into position, trying not to frighten the massive green creatures. When I whispered, "*Go!*" we flung rocks at their heads. Our agreement on the walk over was to focus on the frogs that were floating close to the edge of the pond, they would be easier to drag to shore. Wading into the dark, murky water was not an option for any of us.

Jimmy was the first to hit a target, but not hard enough. Our selection dwindled as we heaved our weapons and missed. The frogs balked and ducked under the surface. Danny finally scored our prey. He carefully aimed, nailing the big guy right between the eyes. The blotchy bullfrog floated to the surface, belly up.

The boys quickly swapped the rocks for the golf clubs and slid the appendages across the tranquil pond. I squeamishly held the edges of the bucket with the tips of my fingers as they carefully dragged the dazed and confused critter, aiming its bulging body towards the opening.

The comatose frog was slimy, thick, and heavier than we anticipated. Most importantly it was alive. I lowered the bucket to let some pond water seep in and covered it with the towel, preventing our catch from leaping to freedom on the walk home.

97

The sky was black, stars twinkling above the golf course. We ran past my aunt's vegetable garden and snuck into our backyard to wash the sludge off our skin and shoes. Danny and I ducked into the back door of our garage. As Jimmy took off for the farmhouse, I told them I owed them one, and I meant it.

Danny placed the bucket on the workbench so the dogs would not bother our catch. I covered the top with an old screen and put rocks on top so the bullfrog could breathe but not escape. I had a hard time sleeping that night in anticipation of the next day's events. Danny and I were both having regrets because we knew our little friend would not live past second-period science class.

I wasn't pleased with my cruel assignment and didn't trust the raucous kids on the bus from interfering. I convinced Mom to take us to school so I could spend as little time as possible with the smelly creature, now in a cardboard box. I reached the lab before the school bell, turned in my homework, excited to be rid of my bounty, and headed to my first period.

If I couldn't avoid the situation, I planned to manipulate it. An hour later, I returned to the formaldehyde-scented lab. The pungent odor was overwhelming—my eyes were irritated, and my stomach flipped. The student's donations awaited their fate, hidden in buckets and boxes on a lab table. Our mad science teacher was fully prepared for our gruesome experiment: knives and long metal pins had been carefully placed on each plastic cutting board.

Frogs were commonly used for teaching dissection, this Catholic nun preferred a more savage method. Sister Lucille taught us about *vivisection*, performing surgery on the living. Her rationale? She wanted us to view the central nervous system and its internal structure, hard at work. Most of us kids were squeamish, and the frogs were dazed and bewildered. I was relieved when she added that it was a group effort.

I chose my colleagues wisely. I sidled up to Donny and Michael, boys that would allow me to take notes. *Anything but the cutting*. Michael's five older siblings had survived this lab assignment, and now it was his turn, he seemed to be looking forward to it.

There was a rumor that Donny tortured animals on the weekends. He was also a diehard KISS fan and never missed an opportunity to frighten a substitute teacher with his blood capsules. He hid the plastic caps filled with red corn syrup in his mouth before class. After writing her name on the chalkboard, the teacher turned to face us right as Donny bit down on his molars, fake blood slowly drizzled down his chin. He added to the show by shaking in his chair, as if he was possessed by a demon. When we had a sub, Donny typically ended up in the principal's office. He felt the performance was worth the punishment. His classmates agreed.

Each trio of students huddled around their workspace, surrounding the patient like surgeons in an operating room. Michael pinned the webbed feet to the cutting board, belly side up, the organs nervously pounding against the wet slippery chest. *Thump, Thump. Thump, Thump.*

I was nauseous, beads of sweat formed on my upper lip and forehead. The pungent smell of methanol permeated the room, it was becoming intolerable. The teacher circled the room, assisting squeamish students. She admired my catch, smirked, and asked Donny to stick a pin into the bullfrog's brain. "He won't feel it," she promised, "It's necessary to ensure there would be no pain when we cut open his abdomen."

A quivering female student raised her hand and asked, "Why can't we do this *after* they're dead, Sister?" The nun returned the question with wild fascination in her eyes, "What would be the *point*? Watching the internal organs fully functioning in a live animal is a fascinating experience." My cohorts didn't seem to mind. They actually appeared to be enjoying themselves.

As we made observations about the experiment, I scribbled notes, breathing through my mouth. The skin was carefully sliced and pinned to the board, exposing the abdomen. I could see the inner workings of the bullfrog. Working in unison like an old timepiece, the heart thumped, blood rushed through the shimmery organs and veins. I excused myself, convinced my breakfast of Eggos with syrup would be revisiting.

I wiped my brow and walked towards the windows for some fresh air. The sociopathic deity asked why I was not at the table with the other children, enjoying the performance of our helpless martyr. I explained that I wasn't feeling well and was afraid I would become ill. Not wanting the return of my starchy breakfast to ruin her lesson plan, she allowed me to use the restroom.

I didn't rush. I was relieved when I inhaled the fresh air, taking deep breaths as I walked down the hallway. I even enjoyed the chill as I passed the first-grade classroom. The girl's lavatory was empty. I splashed cold water on my face and held the sides of the sink to steady myself, willing the food in my stomach to stay its course and finish the digestive process. I slowly regained my composure.

After a few minutes, my stomach obeyed me. I dried my face with the stiff, brown paper towels, the texture of cardboard, and hid in a stall. A female student was finally summoned to check on me. I claimed a stomach ache, so she left me alone.

I had hoped capturing the sacrificial amphibian for my team would make up for the fact that I was not present during its demise. As poorly as I felt, at least my belly would remain intact. Though the pin of guilt had already punctured my brain.

Children of the Cornfield

The Shilling's family farm stood across the street from our house. This was another secret place to cause mayhem after being banished from the barn and golf course. The land used to grow hog corn ran about half a mile alongside Kimmens Road. The farmers said it was a good crop if the stalks were "knee-high by the Fourth of the July." Each year, we patiently waited until we could hide beneath the corn unseen and explore the field.

We ran through the maze as if we were wild animals, zigzagging between the stalks. The challenge was to find our way out and meet back at the clubhouse. That game was never my favorite. My internal compass had never functioned, so I was usually the last to return to home base.

Other days, we found a spot in the corn field, formed a circle, and all leaned back against the stalks, cracking stems to cushion our fall. This created a place for us to sit and visit outside the purview of any adults that may have been interested in our supervision.

Our parents had reminded us several times that the hog corn was not safe for human consumption. Not only was it sprayed with toxic pesticides, but the kernels were also the texture of rocks. That was disappointing.

We had hoped they were the same sugary cobs that grew in the fields of Amish country. The elders sold the ears for a dime a piece, Mom always bought a grocery bag full. We shucked the cobs and boiled them until they were bright yellow. After slathering them with butter and salt, we gnawed on them until our bellies ached.

Grandpa Gossage taught us to act like we were typewriters as we gobbled the kernels from left to right, yelling "*Ding!*" when we finished a row. Corn on the cob night was a rowdy affair in my house.

Confirming our parent's warning, we ripped a cob from its leafy stalk and pulled the husk back revealing a bright orange glow. It didn't crack our teeth when we tried to eat it, but we still spit the kernels to the ground.

An idea was spawned at a Kimmensville Club meeting that would entertain us each fall and wreak havoc on every home within a half-mile radius. We couldn't eat the corn, so we found another use for it. We called it *cornin'*.

By late summer, the stalks bowed from the weight of the cobs, it was finally time to harvest. Every kid on Kimmens was involved in the cornin' escapades, even my cousins joined us on a few early evening assaults.

Colleen, Tommy, and Andy were typically missing from our rogue missions. It wasn't worth the price we'd pay for dragging them along on our naughty adventures. Righteous Uncle Jim could never imagine his kids doing anything wrong without the influence of their older cousins. He was probably right, so we avoided the situation. We justified this scheme as harmless, compared to most days. They were thrilled to come along.

Cornin' involved planning, teamwork, elbow grease, thieving, and the ability to run around the neighborhood at night. If you weren't allowed out past dark, you had to be willing to sneak out. The stealing part was explained to us by Aunt Judi when she caught us picking the corn. She was the first, and the only adult to discipline us for yanking the wagon full of cobs off their stems, knowing they didn't belong to us. She had insisted we wheel the stolen haul to Mrs. Shilling's farmhouse and apologize.

Our heads hung in shame, we reluctantly walked the half mile to Mrs. Shilling's house. We had debated stashing the corn in the field and getting it later since we already picked it. Danny asked, "What is Mrs. Shilling supposed to do with a wagon full of hog corn?"

We had an ulterior motive for objecting to our punishment. None of us kids were interested in confronting the legend of Mrs. Shilling, which included witches and a haunted house. Aunt Judi did not accept our last-minute plea, and we soon found ourselves shaking in our shoes when the witch answered the creaky, wooden door.

Mrs. Shilling peeked through the open crack, not disappointing the image we had conjured up in our creative, little minds. Her gray hair was wound into a bun at the nape of her neck, a black dress hung on her skeletal frame with a gray shawl draped over her shoulders. We mumbled our apologies to the tall, thin woman, pointing in the direction of the wagon.

After a moment of silence, our fingers crossed behind our backs, "We promise we won't *ever* do it again." The group of us turned and walked down the steps. We left the corn piled on the edge of her lawn and pulled the Red Flyer back down her gravel driveway. She just stared at us, never uttering a word.

Although we feared Mrs. Shilling would cast a spell on us, we took our chances and continued to corn houses every fall, but never Mrs. Shilling herself.

After picking the bulkiest cobs on each stalk, the neighborhood clan would gather on my family's front porch. Catching up on school gossip and teasing each other, we shucked the corn into a plastic bucket. The husks and silky strands of hair were tossed into grocery bags propped open on the cement patio. We had saved the corn silk a few times hoping to make a doll with beautiful, golden hair. By morning, the silky threads were always brown and shriveled.

We cracked the ears in half over our knees, twisting the cobs as we flicked the kernels into the bin. The can was half-filled with glowy orange corn, our fingers were screaming. We rested our digits until they would be needed later that evening, after dusk, when the real fun would begin.

The event called for dark clothes with deep pockets. Hoodies became the ideal cover, extra pockets for our stash and a cover for our identity. We met in our garage and stuffed every crevice of our clothing with corn kernels before setting out for Kenyon Road, avoiding our own homes for now.

Everyone knew it was us. For some reason, no one ever called our parents. They were probably happy it was only corn we were throwing.

The poor residents of the duplex near the end of Kimmens were always the first targets. Next, we passed the Jones' house on the corner. The wife gave us epic Halloween candy and cookies with warm cider when we sang holiday carols on their front porch. Not to mention the support she showed for our school fundraisers. No one wanted to stop that cash flow. We moved on.

Turning north on Kenyon, we hit the Wellin house because one of the boys was kind of cute. The next logical mark was Old Mr. Reed. Crouching under windows and behind trees, we grabbed handfuls of corn from our pockets. On the count of three, we bravely tossed the kernels at the windows then took off running. They hit the glass like bullets from a machine gun.

We loved the shock factor it had on our victims. Hearing their screams as we sprinted to the next house, laughing and planning our next ambush. We felt guilty that the homeowners had to sweep their front porches the next day, but not enough to stop.

Two successful attacks gave us the courage to move onto the Lenhart's. We chose our spots behind bushes in the backyard, bordering the course. As we grabbed a smattering of kernels from our pocket, two long-haired, lanky teens ran from their garage. One was holding a basket.

We dropped our weapons as we sprinted towards the golf course, corn falling from our pockets, leaving trails like

Hansel and Gretel. As we ran, we dodged rotten tomatoes being hurled at us like missiles. Sue did not survive the attack unscathed. The spoiled fruit made contact with her bare thigh, a loud wet *"smack"* echoed across the course. *"Ooooouuuuuchhhh! Shit!!"* Karlene chuckled as we zigzagged across the lawn, warding off their shots and hoping they were almost out of vegetal ammunition.

In our backyard under the moonlight, bent over and out of breath, we had inspected the rising welt on Sue's leg. Over the next couple of weeks, it turned various colors and resembled the inside of a jawbreaker. The teen attackers did not intimidate us from hitting their home in future years. We needed retribution for injuring one of our own.

Mom had given us the idea for our next neighborhood prank. She innocently repeated the childhood story of her brothers stretching a roll of toilet paper across a dark road, each holding an end, to scare oncoming cars. The gang thought we'd try it on the few cars that passed down Kimmens.

That evening, clouds had blocked the moon and stars, providing an eerie glow. The group split up between opposite sides of the street, one designated TP holder on each team. Our first startled driver slammed on his breaks and skidded on the gravel. The bathroom tissue snapped on impact. As we scattered and hid, we heard him yell profanities out of the open window.

This particular high jinx, however, was short-lived. Mom had heard the screeches, saw the stream of paper strung across the street, and knew what we were up to. Regretful that she inspired the event, she guilt-tripped us into stopping. Instead, we only stole toilet paper to vandalize trees each fall.

The deep ditch across the street from our homes led up to the cornfield and was a haven for fun in the winter. The ridge transformed into a beautiful snow bank.

After the blizzard hit in 1978, we had climbed the white mound and touched the telephone wires before sliding down. We smiled as Mom took pictures of us in our furry winter parkas.

When the snow was not quite as high, the drift was ideal for protecting one side of the neighborhood in a snowball fight. The whole crew had pitched in to make the second snow barrier in our front yard. After building the wall and forming stacks of snowballs for the impending war, we took a break to thaw our fingers and noses in front of the fireplace.

Mom didn't mind the wet, messy kids traipsing through her house. She often invited everyone in for hot chocolate from Amish country. If we had bread in the house, she would toast a stack and cover each slice with butter and sugar. We dipped our frozen fingers and bread into the warm mugs, traces of butter floating on top of the steaming chocolate.

After hungrily slurping down our hot cocoa, we groaned as we stepped back inside our damp winter snowsuits. Despite placing them near the fireplace, they never thoroughly dried. Shaking off the initial chill, we foraged back outside.

The winners of three rounds of rock-paper-scissors decided our two captains, each choosing a few kids for their army. War was declared! Snowballs were hurled across the street, everyone ducked behind the barricades to shield our noggins. We only paused for the random passing car or when someone cried from getting slammed in the face with a frozen ball of ice.

When the older boys crashed our snowball fights, tears were inevitable. Bobby Lowers and Tom Espinosa would throw those damn snowballs at us as if they were on the pitcher's mound at a high school baseball game.

Bobby and Tom did come in handy for difficult jobs, like the time we built a tunnel in the snow-filled ditch between our mailbox and Karlene's. The teenagers dug for hours as the rest of us shoveled piles of snow out of the way. It was finally complete, but we were afraid to go through the dark channel.

Bobby and Tom assured us they packed the roof tightly and it would not cave in, trapping us in an ice-cold hell. Bobby got down on his hands and knees and crawled through to show us "little chickens" how easy it was. Even though a few moments later he had safely popped out the other end of the long passage, we were terrified.

I stalled as long as I could but felt compelled to at least attempt the feat. The teens went to so much trouble to build it for us. If we refused, we knew a few punches and wedgies were in our near future.

The boys went first, and I followed. Claustrophobia set in quickly. The snow was packed so thick in the middle it was pitch-black. One behind the other, we scampered through the dark tunnel, blind as bats. The sheer adrenaline keeping us going, along with a little help from the person behind us yelling and pushing if we slowed down. Sweating in our snowsuits. It felt like an eternity. When at last we emerged, it was glorious to see the sunlight.

On more innocent winter afternoons, Danny and I loved to rifle through Mom's recipe box and bake. Many weekends were spent making our prized desserts. Mom's collection had consisted of handwritten cards from Grandma Alice and a few recipes cut from magazines.

We made endless calls to Grandma, "How do we convert metrics to standard measurements? Can we use substitutions? What do you mean by *oleo*?" Danny and I took notes. We eventually learned the difference between baking soda and baking powder, to replace buttermilk with whole milk and a splash of vinegar, and that oleo is margarine.

We also experimented with Mom's three-ring *Betty Crocker Cookbook* and invented our own concoctions. If our creation was a success, we printed the ingredients on a card and filed it under the appropriate section in her recipe box.

Our favorite brainchild was Peanut Butter Plopper Droppers. It consisted of peanut butter dough dipped into a bowl of melted chocolate. After bobbing around and completely immersed in the sweet confection, we poked the candy with a toothpick and lined them on a sheet of wax paper to dry. They looked just like the traditional Ohio Buckeye treats, without the circle of peanut butter showing at the top. Danny and I felt this sweet dessert deserved its own label, plus we just liked saying Peanut Butter Plopper Droppers.

Our frequent baking episodes are why Mom had mistaken a clump of mud in a lunch bag for our delicious chocolate brownies. Danny saved his paper lunch sack to collect dirt for a school science project. On the way home, he scooped a moist handful of mud from the ditch, threw it in the bag, and folded the top shut.

We walked in the door as Mom was unpacking groceries and putting them away. Adding to the clutter, we set our things on the counter and poked our heads in the bags to see what she'd bought. Danny, distracted by a box of Twinkies, neglected to see our hungry Mother open his lunch bag. She thought she was in for a treat when she popped a big piece of mud in her mouth and began to chew.

Walking home from school on a day our brother was absent, Sue, Dena, and I attracted some unwanted attention from a group of older boys. We were just feet from the school bus stop when a yellow Gremlin rolled to a stop next to us. A young man leaned out of the passenger window and asked us if we wanted a ride. We instantly recalled the "Don't Talk to Strangers" lecture from school and took off running through the yards screaming *"Noooooo!!"*

Breathless, Sue and I burst through the door and told Mom about our attempted abduction. She walked with us to Aunt Judi's so the adults could discuss what to do next. They were concerned that this had happened in our quiet little neighborhood. Our dad wasn't home, so they decided to alert the local authorities.

Aunt Judi came into Dena's room to see if we were still rattled and to let us know that the police were sending an officer over right away to take our story. Judi advised us to tell the truth, and if we didn't know the answer, we should admit that to the police officer. This was a serious complaint, she did not want us to embellish the story. We all nodded our nervous little heads and watched Judi quietly close Dena's bedroom door.

My cousin's first reaction was to primp before the police officer arrived. She pulled out her stash of dress up clothes and jewelry, and we quickly went to work. We clamped plastic rhinestone earrings on our tiny earlobes, wedged tiaras in our hair, and slid on shiny dresses. We completed our ensembles with feathery pink boas and sparkly heels. Dena suggested the blue eyeshadow and pink blush that we liberally applied to our faces.

Judi yelled up the staircase, the police officer had arrived. We sashayed down the stairs like we were in a runway show, wobbling on our heels. The look on Judi's face was pure horror. The handsome police officer blushed and tried not to laugh. We ignored their reactions. Sue, Dena, and I knew this was important; we were confident we dressed appropriately for the occasion. In hindsight, we most likely looked like drag queens.

The police officer had a harder time getting through the interview than we did. We noticed his giggles and side glances at my aunt. After giving him our best account of the event, he left and promised to follow-up.

True to his word, he called the next day. They had located the vehicle based on our description of the car and partial license plate. The owner was very disappointed in his teenage son who admitted he'd only been joking around with us. The police officer lectured the young man about the seriousness of child abductions, then let him off with a warning. We deemed the officer our new hero.

The residents of Kimmensville were an adventurous and hearty crew. We survived the shenanigans, the cornfield did not. Mrs. Shilling eventually died, and her family sold the land to the highest bidder. The idyllic setting was disrupted. Where the stalks once grew, now stand a series of houses. Sadly, for the next generation Kimmensville Club, the days of cornin' the neighborhood were over.

Lubba Cheekers

Suddenly, we were a family of six. After the drama on the evening of Amy's birth, we welcomed our adorable, little sister home. Balancing on my new crutches and unable to join him, I watched Danny from the picture window. The town crier ran up and down Kimmens Road broadcasting his message, "*I have a new sister!!!*" When he tired, the three of us scrunched together on the couch and cuddled the tiny little person that would occupy one of our rooms.

With only three bedrooms in the house and outnumbered, Danny had to choose a sister as a roommate. We instantly loved our little sibling, but the crying, diaper smells, and lack of privacy would be a challenge. Danny begged Mom and Dad to remodel the basement. They were not persuaded.

Amy and her crib started out in Danny's room. Enamored with our new sibling, Danny could not keep his hands off of her chubby cheeks. Our brother incessantly squeezed, kissed, and blew raspberries on Lubba Cheekers, his affectionate nickname for Amy and her cheeks. He was different with Amy, much gentler. Sue and I were his beloved, older sisters but were so close in age we bickered, wrestled, and teased each other until we almost drove our parents mad.

Amy never found *her* naked dolls dangling from a doorknob in a shoelace noose. Danny had claimed the Barbie hangings were justice for something Sue or I had done to him. He did shave the scented, red hair on Amy's Strawberry Shortcake into a Mohawk, out of boredom. She shed a few tears but still carried her punk doll everywhere.

We had a tremendous amount of fun helping our parents raise our little sister. Dad worked swing shifts and often slept during the day when he wasn't on duty. Mom had her hands full with us, the laundry, shopping, and housework generated by our growing family. We helped out a bit, but like our mom, we mostly neglected our chores for play.

It was common to find piles of clean clothes on the couch, dirty dishes overflowing from the sink onto the counter tops, and toys scattered all over the house. When a friend or the Avon lady called to say they were stopping by, Mom put us all to work.

Danny and I threw toys and clothes into our bedrooms, closed the doors, and ran the vacuum. Sue and Mom stashed the dirty dishes they didn't have time to wash in the oven. On a few occasions, we forgot to unload the dishes when our company left. Remembering only after someone preheated the range and filled the house with the smell of melting plastic.

One morning, Aunt Leanne opened our kitchen door to boxes of cereal strewn across the counter top. Three abandoned bowls sat on the dining room table half-filled with glistening milk. Appalled by our untidiness, she passed by the mess looking for Mom.

Mom was sleeping in, so we decided to play a game with Amy. We were taught to swaddle our baby sister in a blanket like a burrito, tucking the corners in to comfort her. When Danny had commented that she reminded him of a football, an idea was born.

Standing a few feet apart, we formed a circle in the living room. As Sue rocked Amy back and forth, we chanted in unison, *"One, two, three...wee Eee EEE!!!"* She released her into the air, and our one-month-old sister flew towards the sibling on her right. Aunt Leanne had just rounded the corner from the kitchen and saw the baby in mid-air. Her cheeks turned red as beets before she yelled at us to stop our foolish behavior.

Our frantic aunt ran to Mom's room, whipped open the door, and found her sister-in-law asleep. *"Betty!* Do you know what *those kids* are doing out there?!" My mom rolled over, rubbed her eyes, and asked, "Are they playing catch with Amy again?" Leanne gasped and slammed the bedroom door.

Our heads bowed, we watched her stomp past the living room, hands balled into fists, her face still flush. We had listened for the final *huff* and the bang from the screen door before we continued the game. Leanne didn't talk to my mom for over a week.

By the time their fourth child was born, any house rules were nonexistent. We were persuasive kids. To be fair, Mom wasn't aware of *all* of our shady exploits. Like the time we tied six-month-old Amy to a sled and pushed her down the snowy hill. Or our reenactment of the *Flintstones* episode when Barney Rubble had a toothache. Sue was right, the door knob trick worked on Amy's wiggly baby tooth.

She secured the string to our sister's incisor and yanked the closet door shut. A bloody tooth popped out and fell to the floor. We all cheered and then froze in horror as blood gushed from our baby sister's mouth.

Mom also wasn't aware that we taught Amy vulgar songs and nursery rhymes until it was too late. Danny and his school buddy Matt repeated the lyrics to our five-year-old sister until she had them committed to memory. The day their hard work paid off, we all received a tongue lashing on the way home.

Mom was talking to her friend in the check-out line at Bordner's when we shamed her. Danny taught her the rhyme, but Sue and I convinced Amy that the adults would like to hear *Mary Had a Little Lamb*.

Amy approached the chatting ladies and politely interrupted. Smiling, she asked if they wanted to listen to her rhyme. Not able to resist the dimples and adorable gesture, Mom and Peggy encouraged her to continue. Hands folded in front of her, she flawlessly recited the verses, finishing with a curtsy.

Mary had a little lamb
She tied it to the heater
And every time it turned around
It burned it's little peter

We also convinced Amy to answer the phone and greet the caller with, *"It's Doobie time!"* The afternoon she actually did it, our hysteria came to a halt when she handed the phone to Mom and said, "It's Dad." Sue, Danny, and I thought our antics were hilarious. The general public, not so much.

In spite of having a toddler in tow, we continued to frequent the local fast food joints. When it came to nutrition, we were terrible role models. Inducting Amy into the world of greasy burgers, fries, chicken'ish nuggets, hot apple pies, and soft serve ice cream.

When McDonald's had a ten-cent sale on hamburgers, my mom handed us a five, we spent it all. No one spoke as we each ate a few burgers on the way home, polishing off the rest for supper and lunch the next day.

As we drove back from a matinee one summer day, Mom had suggested Long John Silver's for a late lunch. We should have been banned after that visit, but we escaped without witnesses.

The lady behind the counter took our orders for fried seafood plates with hush puppies. Mom paid while we found a booth in the corner. As we chatted about the movie, we gulped our food and washed down our heavy lunches with ice cold pop.

Taking advantage of the free refills, Sue, Danny, and I topped off our drinks. We returned to our table just as Mom was lifting Amy from the high chair. She gripped her torso from the back and wiggled her legs free of the wooden frame. The jostling loosened something other than Amy's legs.

A dozen little balls of feces the size of marbles spilled from under her sundress and rolled across the tile floor. We all shrieked, *"Mom!!"* She finally saw the rainfall of turds pouring from the ill-fitting diaper, it was too late. Not wanting to step on them, my siblings and I froze in disgust. Then, we looked at each other and started to laugh, grateful we chose a booth in the corner.

The dilemma of what to do with the baby excrement lying on the floor was solved by my shameless brother. Between chuckles, Mom suggested that one of us grab a handful of napkins while the others take the baby to the car. She would do the dirty deed. My brother thought Mom's idea would bring more unwanted attention. We were already cracking up like teenagers at the mall.

Instead, he kicked every little ball of poo under the table like he was warming up for a soccer match. Mortified, I ran out the door, Sue and Danny were on my heels laughing like lunatics. Our grinning mother walked out behind us, quickly changed Amy's diaper, and strapped her into the car seat. As Mom jumped behind the wheel, she stated the obvious, "Well, we can't go back *there* for a while."

Mom tried to protect her children's innocence as long as she could; her fourth child would be no different. She had asked us not to spoil the fictitious holiday characters for Amy.

I didn't like the idea of people sneaking into my house while I slept but didn't want to deny the coins and gifts they left behind. I was sure my little sister would feel the same way, so we all went along with the hoax.

The Tooth Fairy wanted her teeth to build a castle in the sky. She left coins in exchange for each pearly white left under a pillow. Front teeth were worth a dollar. We learned not to fool her and passed this intel onto Amy. Danny and I spent hours

115

carefully selecting pebbles shaped like teeth from the side of the street. We woke up the next morning to the pile of gravel still under our pillows.

Not all traditions survived, our parents did their best. When Sue and I were toddlers, Santa brought the entire tree and decorated it while we slept. Mom and Dad barely caught three hours of shut eye before we awoke and wanted to open our gifts. That scheme had only lasted a few years before my parents gave up and told us Santa was too busy to bring trees.

We repeated her fibs, like the time Mom saw Santa's sleigh with eight reindeer take off from the roof of our farmhouse. Complaining that we couldn't fall asleep, Sue and I had our backs to the window when Mom spotted the jolly fellow.

The following Christmas Eve, Mom was getting ready for bed when she heard a jingle. She bolted down the stairs in time to witness a pair of shiny black boots disappear up the chimney as he said, *"Ho Ho Ho."*

We were all fascinated by her stories and believed every word. Until the day Sandy told us that her brother had told her, there was no such thing as Santa Claus. We were hesitant to mention it to our parents. We didn't want to let Mom down. The embellishment she had added to her stories was impressive.

During birthdays and holidays, our mom was also generous in the gift department. More than she could afford to be. In the 1970s, Sue, Danny, and I flipped through the Sears Wish Book and made our Christmas lists. I always included the page and item number to ensure there were no misunderstandings. Thanks to Mom's department credit card, she never disappointed us.

In the '80s, parents stood in long lines and fought each other for the hottest toy of the season. We always made sure Santa brought our little Boo Boo her favorite each year. When she was five years old, Amy wanted the blonde Cabbage Patch

116

Kid that came with her own birth certificate. The next year, it was the coveted blue Goodnight Care Bear. We loyally waited in lines at Kmart, alongside a horde of parents doing the same. When the doors opened, Mom sent us in and headed to the checkout line. After a bit of jostling and wrestling, our scrappy brother nabbed the dolls and Amy's wishes came true.

Danny adored Amy, but their stint as roommates lasted less than two years. My brother and I decided we wanted to share a room. Taking inspiration from a *Brady Bunch* episode, we begged Dad for bunk beds. There were no groovy beds in our future. He bought slabs of wood and followed a plan from the *Reader's Digest Complete Do-it-yourself Manual*. We didn't mind. We enjoyed watching him build something for us and swapped quarters immediately.

Sue had also welcomed the change in roomies. Amy didn't snoop in her drawers and tattle on her when she found something forbidden. I also think my big sister resented me for allowing four baby chicks to take up residence in our bedroom.

I volunteered to take some of the newly hatched chickens home from our latest science experiment at school. Using an empty diaper box as a pen, I cut the lid off, placed straw at the bottom, and bent the neck of my desk lamp over the top to keep them warm. I kept the box clean, but Sue continued to gripe about the odor and the *clucking* at night.

After two weeks, she finally convinced Mom the chickens had to go. It was too cold in the garage or basement, so we offered them to my friend. Lisa had taken a few of their siblings to her farm and agreed to let my chicks join them. A few days later, my buddy told me her dog snuck into the hen house and ate my chickens. I cried a little and secretly blamed Sue.

I was still a tomboy who refused to wear dresses and showed no sign of changing. Danny and I had a blast sharing a room. Amy spent quite a bit of time hanging out with us, laughing at our silly behavior.

We drew eyes on our chins with my mom's makeup, covered the top of our faces with a scarf, and hung upside down from the top bunk. She sat on the bottom bunk and watched our puppet show, enamored with her goofy siblings.

We all enjoyed playing Barbie dolls with Amy in the living room, imitating scenes and characters from TV shows. Long gone was my three-story Barbie townhouse and our dolls.

Sue and I donated our collection to the kids at Epworth Nursery School where Mom had worked as a daycare provider. We placed our treasured Barbie and Ken dolls in plastic bags along with their wardrobes and swimming pool. The Corvette was tough to relinquish, but Sue finally gave it up.

The next day, Mom hauled the toys from her car and surprised the kids. By the end of the week, the entire collection was trashed. I'm not sure she should have shared the outcome with us. The boys ripped the heads off the dolls and broke the car, at the same time the girls "lost" most of the clothes and accessories.

Our little latecomer had to build her toy collection from scratch. No space for a palatial Barbie estate, and frankly no interest in one. We used my parent's collection of vinyl to create homes from album covers on our living room floor.

Propping them against each other, we created a roofless maze, plastic furniture in each chamber. We assisted the dolls as they hopped around the homemade estate, the walls plastered with photos ranging from The Mamas & the Papas and Fleetwood Mac to Barry Manilow and Steve and Edie. We didn't make our selection by musician, although we avoided the intimidating mustache on the covers of the Jim Croce albums. Sue, Danny, and I leaned over the walls and played house with our little sister until she tired of the game and knocked over the albums like dominoes.

Amy had much love and happiness in her young life with the Kimmensville Club watching out for her. When we were sick, our caring little sister returned the favor. Taking charge, she nursed us back to health, brought us blankets, and insisted we lie on the couch and rest.

A TV tray always within reach, packed with tissue, water, orange juice, magazines, and a bell. She borrowed the mini replica of the liberty bell from Danny's dresser and directed us to use it to summon Nurse Amy. My little sister took her role and outfit seriously, an apron was tied around her waist with toy medical gadgets protruding from the pockets. When I was not feeling well, I relished in the attention.

Amy may have earned the nickname Boo Boo because she was the last unexpected Gossage child, she definitely wasn't the only surprise child. I actually think we all were. But, we were certainly wanted.

Amy was our grand finale. She ended up being a godsend for us all, breathing new life into our family and my parents' crumbling marriage. We spent hours snapping shots and burning through rolls of 35 mm film taking pictures of our baby sister making faces when she had gas. Sharing the love and admiration of a child softened us and brought us closer together as a family. Amy's nickname should have been, Our Little Blessing.

Work Hard, Play Hard

Once we reached our teens, my parents encouraged us to look for work. Mom had discovered we were charging after school snacks to her Bordner's account. The security was lax at her favorite grocery store.

There was never a question when we plunked down Ho Ho's, Funyuns, and bottles of ice cold Coca-Cola as we rattled off the line we had heard Mom say on many occasions, *"Please charge it to our account, G24."* They all knew us as "Betty's kids." It worked like a charm until Mom received her monthly bill and the balance was much higher than she expected. The store manager confirmed her suspicions.

Every weekend, we pulled scraps of paper from the Chore Jar. The going rate was fifty cents per task. I didn't mind when Sue chose not to pick anything from the jar because I doubled my income. Though I didn't understand why my older sister didn't want the money. She loved expensive clothes like Jordache and Gloria Vanderbilt jeans, leather jackets, and boots.

For a brief period, Sue, Danny, and I had shared a three-mile paper route that we inherited from Karlene. I wouldn't call it a job, we rarely made a profit. On collection day, there were always a handful of contemptible homeowners that refused to acknowledge our knock. After a few tries, we gave up on the deadbeats and stopped their delivery, taking the loss.

Any spare change we did make was spent at the convenience store we passed on our way home. We basically worked for potato chips, candy bars, and bottles of pop.

Rabid dogs were my biggest fear on the route, they couldn't be avoided. Three different dogs bit Karlene, me, and then Danny. Karlene was attacked by a raging Dachshund that had a vertical jump the NBA players would envy. He seized her upper thigh and hung on while she kicked her leg in an attempt

120

to dislodge the little wiener dog. Besides punctures, he left an enormous bruise on my friend that mirrored a nebula.

My bite was more embarrassing than serious. An Irish Setter was guarding the front yard, barking and pacing back and forth. I had tossed the paper onto the porch and dared to turn my back. I heard a growl right before he chomped down on my right butt cheek. Screaming, I swung around in a circle finally shaking the hound from my rear end.

After Danny had been bitten on the leg riding his bike home, our newspaper delivery career ended. A shaggy mutt lunged at him from behind a bush and sunk his teeth into my brother's right calf. Danny freed his leg and peddled home in pain, blood dripping down his leg, soaking his white tube sock. A few hours later, Dad returned home from the hospital with our sutured-up brother and suggested we find a new job.

Our paper route *should* have ended the day Sue and I, once again, were approached by a stranger in a car. Instead of mocking teenagers, this guy was a creepy exhibitionist.

It was football season, and Danny had practice, so Sue and I split the route that day. Without our brother's help to toss the papers, we were heading home later than usual. After the ritual of fueling our bodies with junk food, we turned left onto Kenyon and started our trek up the hill. Remembering what Dad had taught us, Sue and I were facing oncoming traffic. A red Pinto headed in the same direction slowed to a stop across from us.

Peering out of the open car window was a thin man with brown, frizzy hair and a pointed nose, "Can you tell me how to get to Route 30?" We both pointed south in the direction of the interstate and told him to head that way, he would see the signs. He said he couldn't hear and asked us to come closer. Sue and I hesitated for a minute. We looked for the rare oncoming traffic that passed through the southwest side of Kenyon and crossed the street.

121

His sweaty face was covered in pockmarks, a sinister grin spread across his face. Then we noticed the white T-shirt was his only attire. A wrinkled penis sat between his hairy thighs, beady eyes anxiously focused on our reactions.

We gasped at his pathetic but threatening member, I took off running as if I was competing in a one-hundred-yard dash. Not hearing the slap of Sue's tennis shoes on the tarred road behind me, I turned my head. She was uncomfortably looking away from the offending party while explaining how to find the highway on-ramp.

I stopped in my tracks and swung around. Fists balled, I screamed from the bottom of my gut, *"Ruuuuuuunnnnn!!!!"* The fear in my voice was enough to rattle Sue. She caught up with me about the time the pervert turned his car around and sped off.

My cousins heeded our warnings, but Tommy and Colleen still took over the paper route. I wished them luck and transitioned to a much more lucrative and less dangerous career. Babysitting. Word had spread throughout my neighborhood. I was responsible, cleaned the house, and played games with the kids. I was proud that I had earned a stellar reputation. Some babysitting gigs were more enjoyable than others, I accepted them all.

My three cousins next door were my favorite kids to watch. Since Colleen was only two years my junior, she was my little helper. Aunt Leanne and Uncle Jim did not pay as well as my other customers, but I liked spending time with them. It also gave Colleen and me a chance to torture her brothers.

Our most creative haunting was the day Colleen hid under the bathroom sink. Minutes before I declared bath time, I had distracted my four and seven-year-old cousins. Their big sister cleared a spot next to the Amway shampoo bottles and extra toilet paper rolls. I called for Tommy and Andy and told them their bubble bath was ready.

After grabbing plastic action figures, they stripped down and dipped their toes in the water before completely submerging their bodies in the bubbles. I sat on the toilet seat lid to keep an eye on them, but more so to watch their reaction to the "ghost" in the bathroom.

The top left drawer suddenly flew open, exposing brushes and combs. The small drawer on the right containing toothpaste and floss jutted out and slammed shut. The drawers continued to fly open, closing just as quickly. The boys froze in horror while I played along. My eyes opened wide, I whispered, "What was *that*?" They both shook their heads, stunned into silence. The cupboard doors cracked and swiftly shut, one after the other. Using both her hands and feet, several drawers opened and closed at the same time.

Tommy and Andy huddled in the corner of the tub, legs pulled up to their chest, whimpered and pleaded for it to stop. I continued the charade by acting frightened myself and saying it must be a *ghost*. When they started to cry, I reassured them that the invisible being living under their vanity seemed to have gone away. Colleen's queue to chill out.

The boys jumped from the tub, grabbed their robes, and ran on tiptoes to their bedroom. I wiped down the wet footprints on the floor as I giggled about how brilliantly Colleen performed her part.

I am not sure what I was thinking as their babysitter, as opposed to their cousin, because they wouldn't sleep. What sane person *could* rest after witnessing a paranormal phenomenon in your own bathroom? Worried my aunt and uncle would come home to this, I told the boys about our hoax. They were furious, so now anger kept them from a restful slumber.

I always assumed they tattled the next day. If they did, Jim and Leanne would not have been surprised.

123

One of my most challenging babysitting jobs was watching the son of Mom's PTA friend. It was a decent paying gig, and there were always plenty of snacks, but Billy was karmic comeuppance for torturing Tommy and Andy.

Anne was the oldest child, a wise old soul. She struck up conversations with me, asked personal questions, and complimented my outfits. Her brother was out of control and fearless, a toxic combination for a six-year-old boy.

I questioned the latch on the outside of Billy's bedroom door, six inches from the top of the frame. The lock was intended to keep the high-spirited child inside, the height a testament that his big sister might liberate him. I learned to love the latch. I used it when I ran out of reasonable options for controlling the adorable toe head. Restrained like a caged animal, Billy felt defeated. Under my watch, he ultimately broke free.

The little boy was amped up from the time I arrived and immediately started misbehaving. Within the first hour, he earned a time out. Directly below Billy's bedroom, his sister and I were playing Monopoly in the dining room. Facing the sliding glass door that led to the backyard, I waited for Anne to roll the dice and move her silver cat token when something fell from the second story. I looked up to witness the boy gracefully land on his feet, a quasi-Spiderman, knees bent and fingers sprawled across the grass.

We jumped up, almost spilling our game, and chased him as he sprinted across the backyard towards the Moffitt Heights elementary school playground. It was not an easy feat, but Anne and I finally cornered him. I threw Billy over my shoulder and carried him back to the house, reminding myself to lock his window, as well as the bedroom latch.

On the evenings that I was double-booked with babysitting appointments, I threw my sister a few opportunities. My savings account had continued to grow, I was feeling generous. Watching a kid for fifty cents an hour was *not* her preferred means of making money, but Sue had her eye on a new pair of leather boots, so she caved in and accepted my offers. I was repaid by losing a customer when they returned home early to find my big sister and her friends partying in the living room while their child cowered in his bedroom. Embarrassed when I was scolded by the mother the next day, I surely took it out on Sue.

Babysitting and chores were not easy money but provided a steady income. I opened a savings account and enjoyed seeing the balance rise.

Besides my nest egg, I had a collection of coins that Danny and I discovered by painstakingly searching through the change from our paper route. Swapping the rare coins with one from our pocket, we looked up the estimated value in Danny's copy of the *Handbook of United States Coins*. Our collections included Buffalo Nickels, silver dimes, and silver quarters. We read that if we waited, the value would increase. Deciding to be patient, I placed my coins in a small, white gift box and hid it in the back of my top dresser drawer.

Unfortunately, Sue found my coins. Scrounging through my drawer looking for money to buy cigarettes, she unearthed the box from the corner of my drawer. The fact they were hidden behind my Christmas socks didn't faze her. The old coins were worth over twenty times the amount she spent on the two packs of Marlboro Lights. I discovered the lost coins days later and asked Mom for Sue's allowance until her debt was paid off. Expensive smokes.

We had swapped bedrooms again, and Danny moved back in with our little sister. My parents thought my brother and I were getting too old to share a bedroom, they suggested that teenage girls were a better fit. Sue and I fought on a regular basis, mostly because she wore my clothes without my permission and I relentlessly tattled on her. Danny and I had grudgingly agreed, and he surrendered his lower bunk to Sue.

Sue and I did agree on some things, like the purchase of a new stereo. We pooled our Christmas money and found a silver Technics turntable with the smoked Plexiglas cover and AM/FM radio on sale at Kmart. We planned to put a bulky speaker on each side of our room, the turntable in the middle. Since our taste in music differed so drastically, we bought separate albums.

Thriller was just released, and Danny and I were huge Michael Jackson fans. Not hesitating about splitting the cost, we slid our first vinyl record into the shopping cart.

He and I were captivated by Michael Jackson's dancing. My brother spent hours teaching himself to break dance in his bedroom. After the stereo, he joined Sue and me in our room some nights to entertain us with his moves. Danny would glide across the floor doing the Moonwalk or ripple his entire body down the hallway practicing The Worm. He had a natural rhythm and still spent hours perfecting his moves.

My brother had longed for the red leather jacket with black stripes his idol wore in the *Thriller* music video. Each time he begged for a replica of the shiny coat, Mom told him it was too expensive. Danny didn't care that the attire at our rural school consisted of running shoes, blue jeans, baseball hats, and sports jackets. He would have pulled off the red leather jacket like a boss. Mom wanted to buy it for him for Christmas, she couldn't justify the cost. She had four kids in need of winter clothes and boots.

We all continued to find ways to bring in cash, Sue being the only one old enough to work at a real business. For a few months, she held the mundane task of making salads at a local restaurant. Her title was Salad Girl. Unfortunately for one guest, this was during her Lee Press-On Nail phase.

Sue had tossed humongous quantities of lettuce, tomatoes, shredded carrots, and radishes in a five-gallon plastic bucket. She scooped up bowls of greens and served them to customers as they waited for their dinners. After delivering the

126

salads, Sue noticed a missing red fingernail. My sister anxiously searched the kitchen counter and floor where she was prepping, then traced her steps through the dining room, hoping it popped off as she carried the tray. No such luck. The bright red nail was now masquerading as a crunchy radish slice.

After her restaurant career had ended, she made extra money by grabbing a few slips from the Chore Jar on weekends and offering to do whatever was needed around the house. Sue was creative. Making cash washing Dad's truck, cleaning out the garage, and babysitting Amy. She didn't make any money the afternoon she soaked our living room couch, though.

No one was home to help my big sister drag the dense couch across the living room, or to tell her to stop. The wooden frame was stuffed with cotton filling and covered with brown, burlap-like fabric that felt like a potato sack. She struggled as she pushed it past the dining room and out the sliding glass door onto the deck.

Sue filled a plastic bucket with water as she squirted dish soap into the stream. Using a clean sponge from Dad's workbench, she scrubbed the couch with the soapy water. She was liberal with the bubbles since she was going to hose it off.

The rest of the family returned home and saw the dripping sofa on the deck. Fortunately, my dad wasn't too upset, more mystified why she had thought it would dry out before forming a colony of mold.

My parents weren't prepared to buy a new piece of living room furniture, and Dad refused to use Mom's shiny new J.C. Penney credit card. Uncle Jim, recently divorced and living alone in the big, furnished house next door, gave us his family room couch. The brown, velveteen fabric was patterned with orange and gold flowers and was hideous, at least it was soft.

It was time for her to pursue other employment opportunities. This is where Aunt Margaret came in. My sister preferred lounging in the sun to dealing with snack bar customers, so she earned her lifeguard certification. Margaret was happy to help and immediately scheduled her for summer shifts at the Elms. Sue spent her days mostly reprimanding kids for running. Her worst Elms lifeguard encounter had nothing to do with her actual job.

The day after my sister bleached her dark brown hair platinum blonde, a male employee who had a crush on her picked up Sue and threw her in the pool. As she hit the water, she had a flashback of the warning on the box to avoid chlorine for two full days.

Hours after being assaulted, every short, blonde hair on Sue's head had green tips the shade of a clover. I rolled around on our bedroom floor laughing, tears streamed down my face until I noticed my sister had tears of horror streaming down hers. I dried my eyes and offered to help.

Sue handed me a pair of stainless steel scissors that I used to crudely chop off the green tips, placing the clippings on a tissue. When I finished, the pile of hair resembled a little green haystack.

While Sue avoided the jerk that ruined her do, I ran the snack bar at the pool with Margaret. The cozy space was packed with refrigerators and freezers, a popcorn machine, and glass shelves stocked with candy bars. Margaret and I would maneuver around each other, dodging her spoiled poodle, Benji, as we filled orders for the customers.

Our employment at the Elms Swim Club only lasted three months each summer, but they were better summer gigs than most. If she knew how much I had snacked, my aunt would have docked my pay. Not to mention the beer that the lifeguards smuggled out during my watch and hid under a pine tree until their shift ended. Sue told me to ignore them, so I did.

Margaret was a shrewd business woman. She made me fill out my first 1099EZ Federal Tax form when I was only twelve, claiming my two-dollar an hour income.

With all my odd jobs, I was able to save enough money to buy a red, ten-speed bike and send myself on a cruise to the Bahamas. The satisfaction of a brand-new bike, instead of the used cycles Mom bought from the classified section, didn't last for long. My big sister borrowed it one afternoon, and I never saw it again.

Sue didn't feel like walking the half a mile to her friend's house, so after sprucing up her makeup, she jumped on my bike and headed north on Kenyon. Her friends headed her off and told her to ditch the bike and jump in the car.

Not wanting to hold up the party, Sue stashed my new ride behind a tree and hoped it would be there when she returned. That was not my lucky day. Nor my sister's. Once again, I forced my mom to garnish my big sister's allowance until I was repaid for the stolen bike.

My cruise took place during spring break of my seventh-grade year. I had accompanied my Florida family--grandma, aunts, uncles, and older cousins--from Miami to Nassau, Bahamas. Jeneen was the only teen in the Sulte family that was not allowed to join us because she had been "back talking" Aunt Nancy when the trip was being planned. I was the only one from my family that could afford to join them, so I did.

I flew to Florida and met up with my family in St. Petersburg. Early the next morning, we piled into Aunt Nancy's van and drove to Miami where we hung out at the crowded port for what seemed like hours.

The procession of cruise goers finally boarded *The Flavia* and scrambled for a spot on the deck. As the boat embarked, Dena and I hung onto the railings and waved, imagining we were in the opening credits of *The Love Boat*.

I shared a cabin with Dena at the end of a long, narrow hallway, a floor below the adults. Unbeknownst to them, we ran around the boat flirting with a couple of vacationing thirteen-year-old boys, snuck into the casino, and ordered drinks from the bar.

We tossed our hair as we asked for the only cocktails we could remember our moms drinking. Without any questions, the bartender mixed the pink and green concoctions. Giggling, we carried our Virgin Strawberry Daiquiri and Grasshopper drinks with paper umbrellas back to our room, where Dena and I convinced ourselves we were drunk.

As the boat glided into Nassau, the deck was packed with passengers watching young men jump over the sea wall into the water. We descended the ramp, a wave of warm, humid air hit our faces.

Bamboo huts lined the waterfront, souvenirs hung from the thatched roofs, clothing was stacked on the counter tops. Rows of shacks sold identical wares. Grandma taught us to walk away if they refused to bargain with us. She assured us that if they wanted the sale, the shopkeeper would follow us before we reached the next hut. And she was right.

We bartered with the local merchants, walked through town, and stopped for lunch at Burger King, of course. Later, I would return home with a straw hat and tote bag, *Everything's Better in the Bahamas* T-shirts, and a small jewelry box made from sea shells for my mom.

We all signed up for the Night out in Nassau tour for $29.75 each. The package included round trip limo rides to a night club with fire dancers, Calypso singers, limbo dancing, and two drinks. Dena and I were giddy from the lights and sounds of the show, as well as from sneaking a few sips of Grandma's 7 and 7. I swayed in my seat listening to the Caribbean music and watching the dancers, as well as my older cousins. Bobby and Rod were smashed.

Earlier that day, a cruise bartender served the underage teens whatever they ordered. They worked their way through the entire drink menu. That night, Rod rolled off the top bunk, waking his brother when he hit the floor. At first, Bobby got a kick out of his drunken little brother. Then, it wasn't so funny trying to hoist his limp body back into his bed.

We spent the next afternoon at the secluded Love Beach, surrounded by coconut palms and banana groves. On the white sand beach, overlooking a turquoise blue bay, we ate conch fritters, sipped fruity drinks, and danced along to a steel drum reggae band. It was heaven.

The cruise boat offered a movie theater, lounge shows, and swimming pools. The kids were forbidden to gamble in the casino, but Dena still managed to win fifty dollars.

I initially preferred the pool that had an underwater window that peered into a bar. We did tricks as we swam back and forth in front of the window, putting on a show for the adults enjoying a drink. Dena glided down the slide on her belly, head first, hands clasped overhead. She plunged into the water and did a somersault before kicking her way back up to the surface.

I also slid head first and didn't notice that my bathing suit had fallen down. Flashing my budding chest to the inebriated guests, I was mortified when I looked down and saw my one-piece suit around my waist.

Tugging it back up with one hand, I used my free arm to swim to the ladder and scrambled up the stairs. I grabbed my towel and covered myself, I told Dena what had happened. She giggled as we ran to find a pool without windows.

The buffets were endless. My cousins and I heaped piles of food on our plates, going back for seconds and sometimes thirds.

The final meal of the week was the Captain's Dinner. Everyone dressed up and posed for pictures with the captain, which the stewards hawked to us later for ten bucks a photograph. Grandma bought my shot, as well as our family dinner photo which captured Aunt Judi giving the "up yours" gesture to a snooty waiter.

They served our last, authentic Italian dinner, followed by Baked Alaska. Identically dressed men in tuxedos balanced frozen desserts on trays and paraded around the dimly lit dining room. The sparklers protruding from the meringue tops reflected in the mirrored ceilings. The flames fizzled as the waiters placed a cake at each table, carefully pouring steaming alcohol over the mounds, browning the top. Dena and I were speechless as we savored our decadent dessert. This was a far cry from my old standby, Peanut Butter Plopper Droppers.

The trip came to an end. I said farewell to my Florida family and returned home with my souvenirs, glowing suntan, memories of my adventure across the Atlantic, and an extra eight pounds of weight.

I was proud of what my hard work had provided me. Mom may not have spent much time disciplining us, but she taught us the importance of working hard and how to enjoy what we had earned. And then some.

Teen Angst

My older sister and I enjoyed similar interests this time around as roomies, sharing things like the stereo and the baby blue Princess telephone we received for Christmas. When we weren't calling our friends, the three of us used it to prank people.

Sometimes the Kimmensville kids joined us, everyone sitting cross-legged on our twin beds as we schemed about our next call. One of our antics was to dial random numbers and ask the person on the other end, "Is John there?" They mostly replied, "No, I'm sorry. You must have the wrong number, there's no John here." Stifling our laughter, we demanded, *"Then what do you pee in?! A Dixie cup?!"* We always hung up before they could answer.

Sue and I also looked forward to Saturday mornings. Stretched out on our mint green carpet with my sister's cassette recorder and a few blank tapes in front of us, we listened to Casey Kasem spin our favorite songs. Since our music preferences differed considerably, we mixed our own recordings as we listened to the *American Top 40* host count down the most popular songs on the radio. If we were fast enough and stayed silent, we recorded our tunes without Casey Kasem's or our own chatter.

We also both enjoyed listening to the long-distance dedications sent in by a separated loved one. Casey always followed the reading with a fitting song. Danny did an excellent imitation of Casey's cheesy sign-off, *"And don't forget, keep your feet on the ground and keep reaching for the stars."*

The wall on Sue's side of our bedroom was plastered with glossy posters of Van Halen and KISS, including a close-up of Gene Simmons and his long, pink tongue. A shirtless David

Lee Roth chained to a fence and wearing only skin tight, leather pants adorned the back of our bedroom door until we moved. I carefully tacked pictures of Donny Osmond, Andy Gibb, Leif Garrett, and Peter Frampton on the walls above my bed.

Personal taste aside, we inherited our love of music from Mom. She always had the radio on or an album spinning in the background. Two of her favorite singers were Barry Manilow and Bobby Vinton. Sue, Danny, and I agreed they were pretty corny.

Mom had teased us when my friend was over and made us scream, *"We love Barry Manilow"* before she took us roller skating. To pay her back, Lisa gave our mom a Christmas gift that made her utterly speechless. A life-sized poster from Spencer's Gifts of Barry Manilow in a light blue, polyester pantsuit adorned with rhinestones.

Mom said she loved the print, but wasn't sure they had room on their bedroom walls. My dad shook his head and grunted at the thought of looking at that image every day. Noticing the disappointment on our faces, Mom assured us she would find a spot.

My friend was thrilled when I told her we taped the shiny poster to the back of my parent's bedroom door. Eventually, a shoe rack covered it, but Mom didn't take it down until it began to tear, many years later.

One afternoon, our mom introduced us to a tune that shared her name, *Black Betty*. We didn't care what it meant, we liked the title, and it was fun to sing bam-ba-lam as we tried to keep pace with the singer. We were also children of Betty, so Danny gyrated around the room acting crazy and blind as we all sang the lyrics:

Whoa, Black Betty (Bam-ba-lam)
Whoa, Black Betty (Bam-ba-lam)

134

Black Betty had a child (Bam-ba-lam)
The damn thing gone wild (Bam-ba-lam)
She said "I'm worryin' outta mind" (Bam-ba-lam)
The damn thing gone blind (Bam-ba-lam)
I said *Oh, Black Betty* (Bam-ba-lam)
Whoa, Black Betty (Bam-ba-lam)

Listening to the radio one afternoon, one of us came up with a fun idea. We rounded up the gang and called the local radio station during the song dedication segment. After finally getting past the annoying busy signal, we requested that they play *Black Betty* and dedicate it to Betty Black from the kids of Kimmensville.

Within the hour, we heard the cymbals, drums, and familiar guitar riff blaring from the stereo speakers. We jumped up and down, screaming for Mom to join us as we danced along to the tune. She gave us hugs for thinking of her and danced along with us.

Sue, Danny, and I were slowly transforming into typical sassy teenagers. Our mom was outnumbered three to one. Dad worked endless hours on his shifts at the patrol and taught sharp shooting classes at the Police Academy in Columbus. He also continued to travel the country on hunting expeditions.

Mom tried to make up for our absent father. She hauled us around town and picked up our friends along the way. We loved it when she took us to the Stark Drive-In Theater, always arriving early so we could hang out on the swings before the show began.

The lights would flicker to alert the audience that the film was about to begin. We ran to the car and settled into our seats with the snacks Mom packed to avoid paying the impractical prices at the concession stand. We could sometimes

135

talk her into sharing a tub of popcorn dripping with melted butter, but she pre-planned the candy and drinks.

One night, Mom ventured out to the drive-in with several of our friends and neighbors in tow. As we idled in line, the only adult in the car learned that most of the kids forgot their money. Mom quickly checked her wallet, there wasn't enough cash to cover everyone. Not wanting to deny any of the children, she instructed two of the smaller kids in the back to lie on the floor. The rest of us draped a blanket over them and gently placed our feet on their backs, reminding them not to giggle.

The young attendant had so many heads to count and was distracted by my mom's chit-chat that he didn't notice the lumps on the floor. I'm sure she went to confession the next day.

Mom justified situations like the drive-in as telling "a little, white lie" so she didn't disappoint the kids. But, she did not excuse the day Sue and I got caught shoplifting at Gold Circle. I honestly had never shoplifted before in my life, but after a day at the mall with her friends, I saw my sister come home with a purse full of swag. They usually took small things like makeup and inexpensive jewelry. It added up, and I knew it was wrong, but it was tempting.

I caved in the summer day Sue and I tagged along with Mom and invited Nancy. We each grabbed a plastic shopping basket and told Mom we'd find her later. Sue, Nancy, and I headed for the makeup aisle with the baskets on the same arm as our purses. We casually strolled up and down the aisle and slipped makeup into our purses when we thought we were alone.

My stomach fluttered as I stashed sticky, bubble gum flavored Kissing Potion lip gloss and a tube of black Dial-a-Lash mascara into my bag. I was done, ten dollars-worth of merchandise was all I was willing to take. Sue did a bit more damage, and Nancy was somewhere in the middle.

We asked my mom for the car keys, said we wanted to listen to the radio. She handed us her keychain and promised to be there soon. We walked to the brown Ford in the parking lot, Nancy and I jumped in the back while Sue sat in the driver's seat. We rolled down the windows to get some air and poured the stolen booty onto our laps, admiring our take.

A plain-clothed security guard leaned through the window and flashed his badge in Sue's face. She looked down at the pile of stolen jewelry, makeup, and a box of Lee Press-On Nails and mumbled, "Shit." He stood up, asked us to follow him and bring everything with us.

Sue ditched a handful of jewelry under the seat on her way out, but it didn't go unnoticed by the observant rent-a-cop. He leaned in and grabbed the tangled chains, shook his head, and led us back into the store. The Gold Circle Security team took down two more Gossage teens. Apparently, we weren't cut out for a life of crime.

Sue, Nancy, and I avoided eye contact with the curious shoppers and followed the man to the back of the store. He opened a metal door that led to a small, windowless room with a desk and a few chairs, bright lights beaming from the ceiling.

After piling the stolen merchandise on the desk, he took a seat, and the interrogation began. The guard asked if we were with an adult. We admitted that our mom was shopping in their store, and they had her paged on the intercom, which wasn't unusual.

Mom was confused as to why she was being escorted to the back office. Normally when she was paged at a store, it was because we lost track of her and asked that she meet us at the checkout.

This time, they took her to a room with **SECURITY** stenciled across the door. She scanned the room and saw all three of us sitting in shame, our eyes glued to the scuffed parquet floor, too humiliated to look at her.

She angrily scolded Sue, since this wasn't the first time my sister was caught shoplifting. Then, Mom looked at Nancy and sighed, "*Naaannnccyyy*" as she thought about delivering the news to her parents. Finally, she looked at me with the saddest look I had ever seen on her face. Her mouth formed a frown as she questioned, "*You too, Lisa?! Awwwww...*" My shoulders fell, and my head dropped, I had never felt so ashamed.

The guard tallied up our pillage, but the store did not prosecute. It was now official, all of the Gossage teens were forbidden to enter any Gold Circle establishment for the rest of our lives, or until the company folded in 1988. Mom and Dad also grounded us for a couple of weeks, and Sue had to delay the application for her driver's permit. She was more disappointed about not getting away with the fake fingernails.

Intimidated by our shoplifting experience, we stuck to thieving from the neighborhood, such as borrowing golf carts from the Elms after hours. Weany must have known it was us.

We owned our own golf cart until our cousins Mike and Scott visited from California and ran it over a tree stump. Dad knew it wasn't the first time we took the golf cart at night, and it wouldn't be the last, so he refused to fix the damaged engine and sold it for parts.

That's when we started pilfering from the yard at the Elms. Rows of beige carts were lined up, keys in the ignition, filled with gas, and ready for their morning passengers.

We ducked as we headed for the row furthest away from the clubhouse. Sue released the break and pushed it away from the spotlights, starting the engine after we were a safe hearing distance away. The top floor of the clubhouse was occupied by the greenkeeper, we didn't want him to call Weany.

Typically, the gang just drove around the perimeter of the course, stopping at friend's houses, always mindful of Aunt Margaret and Weany. We were desperate the evening Mom left for work before we had eaten dinner. Pizza sounded good, so we called in our order at LaMoore's Bar & Grill and headed for the golf cart fleet.

Since Sue was the oldest, Danny and I designated her as our driver. She drove us to the far corner of the course and cut across a few backyards to reach Interstate 93. Our big sister checked for headlights, steered the golf cart onto the one-lane highway, and floored the gas pedal. Danny and I grinned at each other, hung on, and screamed, "*Whoooo hoooooo!!!*" as we shook our hair in the wind, adrenaline rushing through our bodies.

A couple of cars passed us during the one-third of a mile ride, they all slowed down and looked, but no one stopped. Sue took a sharp left turn into the parking lot, turned off the engine, and told Danny to keep watch while we picked up the pizza. She didn't want to go inside alone, I didn't blame her, there were always a few seedy customers seated at the bar.

As we reached the golf course, my panic dwindled, and I had an extra-large combination pizza warming my lap. Dad's State Highway Patrol station was only half a mile down the street, I was happy we weren't spotted by a passing cop finishing his shift. Sue darted back across the yards, onto the course, and headed in the direction of Kimmensville.

Instead of carefully returning the cart where we found it, Sue parked in a random spot on the golf course, and we walked home with our dinner. We were always careful not to leave the incriminating evidence too close to our home, we didn't want

Weany to think it was us. Although, I'm sure he knew we were the mystery midnight joy riders.

Borrowing golf carts wasn't the only vehicle exploit Sue and I had in common, we both had memorable incidents with cars. Unlike my older sister, I was incredibly lucky to escape unscathed. Sue had to wait out her shoplifting punishment before she was allowed to apply for her driver's permit. Regrettably, she didn't quite make it before she committed another crime. Three crimes, actually.

Mom was working part-time at the downtown YMCA in the daycare center, and we often rode along and helped out. One summer afternoon, Sue and her friend went along, with no intention to babysit.

They hung out at the YMCA for a bit, not wanting to appear too anxious before asking her for the keys so they could listen to the radio. Mom's car wasn't running properly, so she drove my dad's pickup truck while he fixed her Ford.

Sue and Anita struggled to reach the seat in their tight Jordache jeans, finally managing without splitting the seams. Sue turned on the ignition as she complained about driving a truck, wishing that Mom had driven her car. It wasn't the first time Sue took the cars for a spin. Drivers permit or not, my sister had plenty of practice driving, with and without our parent's knowledge.

Sue's current boyfriend was working at Border's grocery store in Amherst Shopping Center, not far from the YMCA. Sue headed east on Tremont as they listened to their loud music, singing along to the heavy metal lyrics, bouncing off of the truck seats whenever she hit a pothole.

Five minutes later, Sue and Anita pulled into the parking lot and looked for the bag boy with broad shoulders and long hair, resembling a model on the cover of a romance novel.

Sue was distracted looking for Dan when she took a right-hand turn down an aisle, and drove over the back of a car, crushing the trunk. In the process, she also scraped and dented the entire passenger side of Dad's truck. The tires landed back on the ground with a jolt, tossing the unbelted teens around the cab.

The unlicensed drivers panicked. They took off and drove back to the YMCA hoping no one saw what had just happened. They didn't hurt anyone, and most drivers had insurance to cover the cost of accidents, they rationalized.

Sue was so angry at herself for not paying closer attention, and Anita was worried her parents would find out. My sister sped down Lake Avenue in the direction they had just come from, afraid to stop.

Safely parked back in the YMCA lot, Sue and Anita covered their mouths with their hands, staring in horror at the carnage. White paint from the victim's car covered the length of the truck. There was one dent that started on the passenger side door and ended at the rear of the back panel. It was a mess.

At least they found the same parking spot open that they had just vacated. They needed some time and an alibi, they weren't ready to admit what had just happened.

Sue and Anita casually returned the keys to Mom's purse and then played with the kids demanding their attention. When Mom's shift ended, they held their breath as they walked to the truck, the crushed side hidden from Mom's view. Sue carefully opened the passenger door while Mom jumped behind the wheel without noticing the damage. They decided not to mention the accident until they figured out what to tell her, secretly hoping the dents could be blamed on someone else.

Sue and Anita's prayers were answered. Mom said she had to run into a grocery store on the way home to grab a few things for dinner, and it wasn't the store they had just fled.

Mom drove across town and parked the truck, never turning around as she headed in to do her shopping. Sue and Anita wandered over to Baltzly Drug Store and walked up and down the aisles whispering about their mishap, wondering if anyone saw them. It was inevitable that Mom would see the marred truck as soon as she walked out of the sliding glass doors.

They didn't need to own up to the collision. Shaking her head, Mom left the shopping cart full of bags next to the truck, walked to the pay phone attached to the brick building, and called the police. She was put on hold for a few minutes after she reported a hit-and-run and provided the details to the dispatcher, including the description of her vehicle, and the license plate number.

A police officer picked up the phone and frankly informed her that it was *her* that was wanted for fleeing a crime at Amherst Shopping Center. Denying the claim, explaining she was at work all day, Mom was annoyed at the insinuation. The cop begged to differ based on the calls they received about a bronze-colored Ford pickup truck with identical license plates recklessly leaving the scene after running over a parked car.

Mom continued to deny the charges and called her husband to see if he could talk some sense into his cohorts. Dad and a police officer arrived fifteen minutes later, Mom still insisting there must be a mistake. The officer said he had to take Mom to the station for questioning and to complete a written statement.

Dad wasn't sure what to believe but knew his wife was an honest woman and owned up to all of the other accidents she caused, why would she not be forthcoming about this one? It didn't make sense to either of them.

Dad dropped Anita at her house and drove Sue home in Mom's Ford. After spending the afternoon tuning the engine, now he had another car to deal with. Sue sheepishly walked into our bedroom, I asked her what was going on. I heard Dad curse after receiving a phone call, storm out the door, and jump in the car.

I knew Sue had gone to work with Mom that morning, but I couldn't fit the pieces together or figure out the cause of the chaos and why she was returning with Dad.

I asked her, "Where is Mom?" Sue gave me limited details, saying the truck had been hit while parked at a shopping center. Then, she fast forwarded to the fact that our mother was being questioned at the police station for a hit-and-run at Amherst.

My instincts kicked in, as well as the fact I knew my older sister better than most anyone. I asked her if she did it. I knew her boyfriend was a bag boy at the same shopping center, not far from the YMCA. She didn't answer me.

I jumped off my twin bed and shoved my big sister across the room, *"You did it! You took the truck and wrecked it! How could you let our mom go to jail?!"* I jumped on top of Sue, we rolled across the room punching each other. Sue's blows were defensive, mine were angry.

My wild imagination conjured up an image of my mom locked in a cell surrounded by metal bars jutting from the cold concrete floor. We toured the jailhouse and courtroom during a school field trip, the damp image of the cell blocks stuck with me. I imagined her terrified as she sat on a cot shoved in the corner of a cell next to a toilet.

Sue started to cry, finally admitting it was her and Anita. I let up on the beating. She didn't know what to do when they hit the car because she didn't have a driver's license. They also didn't think anyone saw them, so they took off. She didn't want Mom to take the blame either, but she was afraid to admit what she had done and the repercussions she would face. Sue wasn't sure who she feared most, the police at the station or the one that was raising her.

I ran out of the room, found my dad, and told him everything. He looked at Sue like he wanted to shake her. Instead, he dropped his head for a moment and then yelled at her, "Get your *ass* back in the car!" For a second time that afternoon, he peeled out of the driveway, tires screeching as he headed east down Kimmens towards the police station.

Dad returned to the house, this time with my sobbing mother. I was afraid for Sue when Dad yelled that he was pressing auto theft charges against his oldest daughter for taking his truck without permission.

This would be in addition to the other two indictments the police department was charging her with--driving without a license and hit-and-run. Dad added, "*I told them to lock her up and throw away the key*!!" He stormed out of the garage door and headed to his den. Mom and I exchanged worried glances, we were anxious to have Sue home again.

A couple of hours later, quietly this time, Dad backed the Ford Fairmont out of the driveway and returned to the police station to retrieve his daughter. His conscience got the best of him, and he was sure the fear they instilled in her would teach her a valuable lesson.

He not only dropped the auto theft charges, but he also used his influence and connections to eventually expunge the other charges from her record altogether. Sue's punishment included community service and another year of bumming rides from her friends and me. She was eighteen before she drove legally.

My first brush with the law could have been dreadful, it was only two months after I passed my drivers exam. Luckily for me, my dad had been promoted to sergeant at the Ohio State Highway Patrol and had seniority over the trooper that eventually stopped me.

The officer wasn't listening to my excuses as he madly scribbled out a speeding ticket, with probably a few other infractions. He didn't appreciate having to use the bullhorn demanding that I pull over as he chased me through Belden Village Mall.

Stacy was in the front seat using the rearview mirror to apply her makeup when the lights were apparently flashing behind me. Dawn and Nancy were in the back with a case of cold beer at their feet, purchased with Nancy's fake ID. My brother's boom box was wedged between them blaring Bon Jovi. We were all happily seat dancing and singing along, oblivious to the attention I was drawing from the passing cars.

I finally heard an angry voice over the music, *"Brown Ford Fairmont! Pull over, NOW!!!!"* There was no doubt in my mind which vehicle he was pursuing. I grabbed the mirror from Stacy and adjusted it, red and blue lights reflected in my face. I yelled to Dawn and Nancy, *"Turn the music off and cover the beer!!"*

My heart was pounding, my upper lip started to sweat as I pulled off of Whipple Road into the Sears parking lot mumbling, "S*hit, shit, shit, shit, shit.*" The only other thought going through my head was, *Dad is going to be so mad at me.*

I opened the door and got out to prevent the officer from seeing the beer on the floor behind the driver's seat. Bad move

145

on my part. He firmly asked me to get back in the car and hand over my license and registration, as he began writing up my ticket.

"I would have stopped," I explained. "I couldn't see anything out of the back window, I didn't notice the flashing lights. And, our music was so loud I didn't hear your sirens," I pleaded with the irate trooper. Clearly, this wasn't helping.

He was not accepting my explanation, I had to up my game. I casually asked him, my sixteen-year-old attitude in full check, "Do you know my *father*, *Sergeant* Steve Gossage from the Wooster Patrol?" His pen stopped and hovered over the pad. He returned my snarky attitude, asking if I knew my dad's badge number. I didn't but made a mental note that I should find out.

The officer stomped back to his patrol car and picked up his radio, calling the dispatcher to confirm my story. A few minutes later, the trooper returned with an imposing glare, ripped off a yellow sheet of paper with the words WARNING imprinted on the top, and shoved it through the window.

His parting words were, "I suggest you tell your dad about this before I do." I was in utter shock that we got away, I dared not celebrate our scrape with the law until we were safely out of his eyesight. I started the engine and slowly drove back towards Whipple, signaling and coming to full stops. I pointed the boxy Ford to our original destination--a party in Canton.

I wasn't sure who the cop was, so decided I should mention it to Dad. I waited until he was in a good mood the next afternoon, tinkering in the garage on his day off. I wrung the ticket in my sweaty palms as I told my story.

"I had a lack of visibility in the rearview mirror and loud music," I explained. "I should have been more responsible." Downplaying the event, I quickly jumped to the end where the trooper gave me a warning because I mentioned my father's name. I knew boosting Dad's ego and complimenting him was the way to go in this situation.

He laughed as he smoothed his hair in place and asked with a smile, "Do you know the trooper's name?" I read the signature on my warning ticket; Dad grinned and chuckled in recognition.

Mom and Dad were oblivious to most of our mishaps, but they certainly saw a change in all of us. As much as they loved their children, they could not deny the alien abduction that occurred during our teen years.

One day we were sweet, laughing children that adored hugging and kissing Mom while exclaiming our undying love. The next, we were asking her to drop us off a block away so no one would see she was our ride. She must have been heartbroken over her little traitors, especially the day Mom took us to the movies with her new friend.

We were very curious when Mom said Brenda performed in a circus, in addition to her part-time job at the YMCA. Her shtick at the carnival was apparent to us when we saw the woman. Brenda was just shy of four feet tall and struggled to reach the front seat from the curb.

Sue, Danny, and I were lined up in the back giggling. We could only see the tips of her hair over the leather seat, her voice was small and squeaky as she greeted our mom and turned to wave at us. Being the little punks that we were, we did not consider her disadvantage and instead chose to imitate her.

We slunk down in our seats and raised our hands, keeping our elbows to our sides, waving our fingers in the air, and making funny faces. Mom's glare in the rearview mirror should have bored holes through our heads, but we kept snickering and elbowing each other all the way to the movie theater.

Mom was grateful that we preferred to sit away from her. She and Brenda grabbed seats in the back, we gravitated towards the front row. We were still laughing, our mom befriended a little person from a circus, and we were spending the afternoon with her.

Mom never judged people, and she appreciated diversity. She attracted all sorts of interesting characters, including her friend Orpha the janitor at the YMCA with six fingers on one hand. Orpha visited our house one afternoon, and we could not stop staring at the extra digit. Orpha was also parked in our driveway when we returned from the hospital the morning Danny had passed.

After the movie had ended, we all climbed back into the car claiming our same seats. Mom dropped her friend off, we all sat up straight, smiled, and waved goodbye as if we had just behaved like the Von Trapp children all afternoon. Mom was silent as she stoically drove down Lincoln Way with her lips pursed and her eyes squinted, darting straight ahead.

Unlike her typical mood, Mom did not discuss the movie or offer to stop for a treat on the way home. We were uneasy with the silence and started to worry that maybe we crossed the line. Brenda didn't see us, so why did it matter? We soon realized that we thoroughly disappointed our big-hearted mother. Then, one of us made a comment about her little friend, and that was her breaking point.

Our mom pulled the car over to the side of the road, screeched to a halt, and firmly but calmly said, "Get out." Sue, Danny, and I looked at each other in confusion and wondered who she was referring to. She repeated her demand, louder this time, "Get out of my car, *now*!!" We protested and asked why she was doing this since we were miles from home.

She honestly answered it was because she didn't raise us to be ungrateful, inconsiderate, rude, little brats and frankly didn't want to be around us right now. For the third time, our mom asked us to leave. We reluctantly scooted out one at a time, quietly closing the car door right before the tires squealed from the pressure she put on the gas pedal in her hurry to escape us.

My siblings and I stood there for a moment, wondering if maybe she was taking a spin around the block, to teach us a lesson and would eventually come back to reclaim us. After a few minutes, we realized that was not going to happen.

We started walking in silence, staring at the ground and reflecting on our poor behavior. Sue, Danny, and I climbed the hill on Kenyon, we were less than half a mile from home. Thoroughly exhausted and regretful for embarrassing Mom, we had no right to make fun of someone because of the way they were born. Her plan worked, we were nothing but remorseful when we opened the door to an empty house.

If Mom drove straight home, she would have arrived over an hour ago. Our imaginations went wild, we began to worry. What if she decided not to come back? We quietly made a snack, cleaned up after ourselves, and made an effort to tidy up the house, so it was nice when, if, she came home.

A few hours later, we heard the rumble of the old muffler, all three of us sighed in relief. My siblings and I knew our punishment was not over, but at least she was home. She didn't need to scold us again because we immediately admitted our mistake and apologized profusely as she nodded her head in agreement. We were still grounded for the week.

During Aunt Judi's next visit from Florida, she pulled Sue, Danny, and me aside by our shirts after listening to us disrespect our mother. She bent down and pointed at us with her angry finger as she made eye contact with each of us. The frown on her face looked like she had just sucked on a lemon.

She basically told us we were a bunch of ungrateful little shits and she was not going to allow us to treat her sister that way. She reminded us that Betty was *her* sister long before *we* were around and we had no right to treat her sibling this way, she was not our property to abuse. Judi was absolutely correct, but it wasn't something we were used to hearing from our dear aunt. Once again, we knew we had pushed the limit. We apologized to Judi and lied when we promised her that we would stop sassing Mom.

Our mom was so unselfish and giving, she continued to do things for us in spite of the way we treated her. We loved her dearly, but the teenage alien abduction was still in progress.

Her adorable little angels no longer crawled into bed to snuggle with her at night when Dad worked the midnight shift. Instead, we rolled our eyes when she showed us affection. She must have been crushed. Mom continued to accommodate our absurd requests, even when they were not entirely legal.

Sue, Danny, and I had attended a Friday night Massillon Tiger football game. Football was sacred in our little, steel-industry town, everyone showed up for the games. The local businesses shut down early so the employees could attend the home games of one of the winningest football teams in the country.

The school Booster Club gave every newborn male in Massillon a plastic football with Obie, the school mascot, emblazed on the front. The boys were raised playing football or believing they should have played. Friday nights were always a good time in Massillon. We were very proud of our Tigers.

After the game, we walked to Burger Town along with our friends and most of the local teenagers. The place was packed with fans dressed in orange and black gear, every table overflowing with loud teens, groups of kids loitered outside.

When it was time to go, I neglected to check in with my siblings. We each promised four kids a ride home. All fifteen of us met at the Burger Town sign. We asked our friends if anyone had another way home, they all shook their heads. I knew my mom well enough not to panic, she would think of something.

Mom arrived at the fast food restaurant a little later than we agreed, but we expected that. The long, brown Ford LTD barreled into the parking lot, she rolled down her window when she saw the mob of kids. Mom raised her eyebrows and bit her lower lip before she asked us, "How many kids?!"

We all three pleaded and promised that we'd figure out a way to fit everyone. This was before seat belt laws were passed, but obviously carrying fifteen passengers was not legal. Mom, being the pushover that she was, didn't hesitate when we told her they would be stranded if we couldn't drive them. She shook her head and said, "*Pile in!*"

The two biggest kids sat in the front seat with Mom, along with one skinny girl that would duck if we passed a cop. Sue volunteered for that spot. That still left twelve. I jumped in the roomy back seat with three other kids that lived near us, so we didn't have to unravel from this tangled mess at every stop. Another four kids sat on our laps, wedging their limbs into any crack they could find. With each additional body, the car sunk deeper and closer to the concrete. Mom worried she wouldn't be able to drive it.

The groping jokes had begun before we had our third layer in place. Everyone inside was laughing and screaming *"Ouch! That hurts! Get off of my foot."* Only three kids would fit

151

in the third row, but they had to duck their heads, leaving one remaining person, Jimmy.

Someone brilliantly suggested closing the back door, rolling down the window, and having Jimmy jump through the opening. He could lie on the pile of teenagers. Mom's eyes were wet with tears from the clown car routine she was witnessing.

We accomplished our challenge when Jimmy stepped back and took a running dive through the open window, onto the sea of bodies. Us kids on the bottom screamed while the third row drummed their hands on Jimmy's butt and tickled him.

Mom asked, "Everyone in?" When she heard a unanimous "Yes!" she asked who lived the closest so we could drop the kids off in order. She also assured us she would take the back streets to avoid any attention, as she scraped the muffler exiting the lot. "Get comfortable, kids!"

Mom and the fifteen of us survived the trip without a ticket, accident, or parent scolding. Mom quietly coasted into each driveway, we dislodged our friends, waved goodbye, and repacked the car providing a bit more relief at every stop.

After every child had been safely returned home, we thanked Mom profusely. She suggested, and we agreed, that no one mentions this to Dad. He wondered why he had to replace the shocks on the car much sooner than usual, but it was better this way.

Dad was not as trusting and gullible as our mother. He wouldn't have survived thirty years on the police force with her demeanor. Dad once described his career as spending three decades with the scum of the earth and dead people. Those deadbeats ruined it for us when we wanted to pull a fast one on our parents. Dad did not entirely trust his three teens and was aware of the lack of oversight provided by his wife. His suspicions were warranted.

On the weekends, our friends with strict curfews stayed overnight at our house. Dad would come home from his midnight shift and find sleeping bags scattered about the living room. Still clad in his uniform, he walked between the snoozing bodies, beaming the long, silver, patrol-issued flashlight directly into our faces. Waking Dawn from a bed check, my father was greeted with the question, "What the hell are you doing?!" He wasn't always thrilled with our teenage attitudes or our friends.

A benefit of being a second child is the advantage of learning from the mistakes of the eldest. I was astute enough to notice the error in her ways but also took mental notes along the way.

Sue knew I was also deviating from the rules, she still wouldn't let me hang out with her most nights. Though she didn't mind asking me to cover for her when she was lying to our parents about her plans. Since I used to squeal on her, this alone was a leap of faith. Things were changing.

Over time, deceiving our parents, my big sister and I became a good team. I helped Sue sneak out of our bedroom window to go to parties. A few hours later, when I heard a tap on the glass, I pulled her back in. She told her rides that she lived in the house next door. Instead of alerting Dad with headlights beaming in our front window, Karlene's parents would peek out the curtains to investigate the late-night visitors.

One audacious, underage drinking stunt was spawned from sheer boredom. Sue bought a six-pack of beer from the convenience store in town that rarely checked IDs. She had stashed the bag in the garage with plans to smuggle the brews into our bedroom. I got the impression Sue had done this before.

She took a basket of dirty clothes to the basement and returned with clean clothes that were always lingering in the dryer. It was a perfect cover. She snuck the cold brews right past our parents. They thought she was voluntarily doing laundry and smiled.

When Sue turned eighteen, the legal drinking age in Ohio at the time, she shared her license with me. We both used it to gain entry into The Galaxy dance club in Canton, sometimes on the same nights. If Champion was performing, you could guarantee my girlfriends and I were in line, dressed in 80's attire, our over-processed hair adorned with headbands and lace bows.

As many risks as I took, I could not get caught doing anything stupid if I wanted to play sports at Tuslaw. Our high school coach was a tough woman, and I had no intention of crossing her. Dressed in polyester track suits, Coach Wags had the respect of every girl on the team. She was brutally honest, cared for each of us, and knew when we needed help.

As a third baseman, I learned to catch fastpitch softballs relatively quickly, my post being halfway between third and home plates. If I didn't, Wags said I'd get hit in the face quite a bit. And when I did, she'd make me scream, "I love pain!" and run back to my position. The way she went about sharing her wisdom was rather unique, but it worked for us.

Another strong role model and mentor, Wags was there for me when I needed advice, a kick in the butt, or a laugh. She helped me stay on track and focused, right about the time I started to drift.

Danny was also growing up. By the time he was thirteen, most of the calls made to our household were from young girls with high pitched voices asking for "Dan." Our teenage brother was also sporting a soft, fuzzy mustache that covered his upper lip. Danny's thick, silky, black hair hung in his eyes most of the time. He nonchalantly swung his head to the left, tossing his long bangs. Lucky to inherit Grandpa Howard's tall frame, dark eyes, cleft chin, and deep olive skin tone, Danny's features were striking as he matured into a handsome young man.

My brother was not only good-looking, but Danny was also a natural athlete. He grew up playing sports for the school and city leagues. Often nominated as a captain of his basketball and football teams, he led his team to many victories but wasn't competitive himself. Danny enjoyed the camaraderie of his teammates more than the wins.

His good looks and athletic ability were complimented by his sense of humor and intelligence. My brother earned straight A's all throughout school while continuing his quest to give the teachers a hard time. Danny was also budding into a fine artist. Sue and I were fascinated that he spent more time sketching than doing homework, but brought home report cards that far surpassed Sue's and rivaled mine.

He was also becoming a bit more solitary. Danny spent most of his evenings drawing, listening to music, and dancing in his bedroom, but still maintained his friendships and good grades. My little brother appeared to have the whole package. No one noticed the sadness that was brewing inside of him.

Until We Meet Again

Our childhood was so magical, we were blinded by the green grass and the sunshine and neglected to see the storms approaching. I was aware that the kids in the neighborhood were growing up, and the parents were aging, but I never fathomed how much change would enter our familiar world.

The older siblings of Kimmensville took off for college or started full-time jobs. While Sue and I missed our clubhouse meetings, we embraced our teen years a bit too enthusiastically.

Her sophomore year, Sue began spending time with a particular boy at school. Mark was a junior at Tuslaw and had an identical twin brother. Both were famous for their decked-out monster pickup trucks and for switching classes and never getting caught. Undeniably cool kids to everyone who knew them.

The oversized wheels on Mark's ride made it almost impossible for Sue to reach the cab wearing a tight pair of blue jeans. This was a problem considering they were the norm for the girls of that time. Right before we put them on, we popped our clean jeans into the dryer. If we needed to lie down on the bed and pull the zipper shut using a wire hanger for leverage, Sue and I were satisfied.

Mark became a regular around the house. We were used to hearing the roar of his truck as he picked up Sue every morning and dropped her off every night. When Mark wasn't at school or with my sister, he worked at his family's auto shop business.

The spring of 1983, Sue realized something was different with her body. She should have started her period by now, and her chest was tender, she ignored the signs for another month.

Being a nosy and observant sister, I asked why she wasn't using the feminine products from our stash under the bathroom sink. Our mom's version of sanitary pads looked like a small canoe, so we insisted on our own teen supply.

After confronting Sue with my suspicions, she shared her instincts with me. That week, she bravely drove herself to the Planned Parenthood in Canton. Less than one hour later, the nurse confirmed my sixteen-year-old sister's pregnancy.

Sue was afraid to say anything to her boyfriend. First, she shared the news with her usual partner in crime, Anita, who cried with her.

Dread overwhelming her, Sue knew she had to tell Mark. That night, he picked her up for a date, she dropped the bomb before they left our driveway. Mark panicked. He abruptly suggested they both go home to think about things.

When they next spoke, he seemed distant and distracted. My sister was terrified that she was going to be forced to deal with this incredibly, mature situation alone.

Her fears were soon confirmed. Mark began raising hurtful questions about whether he was the father. The scared, little boy turned into a giant coward. He turned his back on Sue and his child, refusing to admit or own up to his responsibilities.

Mom cried, and Dad shouted, the reactions Sue had anticipated. She had just told our parents she was carrying their first grandchild, Mark denied all involvement, and Sue wanted to keep it anyway. She was a tough, young girl. The battles and choices Sue made before her seventeenth birthday would change our lives. Especially her unborn child's life.

Mom had insisted we welcome the new baby into our family. She knew it would be financially difficult to feed the seventh mouth, but she wanted to support her grandchild. Sue was still a child herself. Dad argued, their youngest was only five years old. We were already out of bedroom space. Not the devout Catholic that our mother was, Dad dared to suggest alternative methods available to unwed mothers.

Sue emphatically disagreed about her options. She was having this baby, with or without her family's support. My sister swore that she would do anything to make sure this child saw the light of day. Danny and I were stunned at her bravery, for once we were speechless. We were also frightened about the destiny of our first niece or nephew.

Sue's baby bump began to show, and kids at school were making comments, then rumors began to swirl. Summer break didn't start for two more months. Sue was already feeling uncomfortable going to classes. She also had to watch the guy that was denying his own child move on with his life. Sue was heartbroken. She finished her sophomore year of high school five months pregnant.

Mom had been in constant communication with her mother and two sisters in Florida. She solicited advice and welcomed the comfort. They decided that Sue would spend the summer with Mom's family while they figured things out.

My sister packed the baby blue, hardtop suitcase with any loose-fitting clothes hanging in her closet. As she left our room, I asked her when she was coming back and what would happen to the baby. She said she wasn't sure about anything. I could tell by the fear in her eyes that it was the truth.

Quiet gloom hung over our house that summer. Our neighborhood friends also felt Sue's absence. We all tried to carry on with our lives, the sadness undeniable. Danny and I were afraid to ask our mom about the future of Sue and her baby.

Then, we heard her on the phone talking about a lady that Aunt Nancy knew from work who wanted to adopt a child. The story slowly unfolded.

Aunt Nancy was an RN in St. Petersburg. She worked with a woman who was on an adoption waiting list. Kathy and her husband, Ron, had already adopted a little boy and now wanted a second child.

Kathy brought her excitable toddler into the hospital where he charmed the nurses and frightened the doctors. She claimed they were in their early forties, Ron had a steady job working in management at a big company, and all that was missing was a sibling for Keith and a second child for them to love. Most of what she said was true.

Mom shared this information with Sue, as an option. If Sue chose adoption, which is where the tides were turning, my sister insisted that she would pick the parents. Anonymous adoption centers were out of the question. She secretly hoped to meet her child again and wanted to be a part of their life. She needed to know where the baby was and that it was safe. The prospective parents seemed agreeable to an open adoption.

Aunt Nancy birthed half a dozen kids and raised them with the love of her life. As a nurse, she treated thousands of patients, fulfilling her passion and desire to help people. Nancy was doing nothing less when she put Kathy in touch with my family.

Mom agreed they were a fine choice if she had to make one. The proceedings began immediately. Kathy and Ron hired a lawyer to handle the paperwork and covered all out-of-pocket costs. It was that simple--on paper.

The adults had kept the adoption decision from Danny and me. One week before her junior year of high school was scheduled to start, Sue returned home. She wore her white strapless sundress, a bright pink and blue belt wrapped around her bulging waist. The dress and belt were baggy around her frame when she left. When Sue bent over to place her suitcase on the floor, the fabric pulled at the seams. Danny and I shamelessly stared at her belly. Fascinated that her skin could stretch that far and that a small child was forming inside of our sister.

We begged once again to keep the baby, promising to help raise it. Mom's eyes filled with tears, she broke down and told us what they had been struggling with all summer. Sue added that she only agreed to the adoption because the mother worked with Aunt Nancy and went to Grandma's church. She knew the Florida family would keep tabs on her baby.

Sue couldn't stop wondering what would have happened if Mark had handled things differently. *Damn it!* If only she was a little older and could support herself. It broke her heart to see other soon-to-be mothers plan the upcoming birth of their children with joy, while she prepared, not of her own volition, to give hers away.

My loving mother convinced our dad to hire a tutor. She wanted to shield Sue from the inevitable glares, teen judgment, and snickers from the shallow classmates. My sister was dealing with enough stress for a junior in high school. Mom hired Mr. Miller. Unbeknownst to my parents, he was a hot, drunken mess.

We watched him waddle from his rusted Chevy every weekday at half past three. The soft man with a comb-over, dressed in a polyester suit and stained shirt, knocked on our front door. Danny and I scattered. Sue had told us he reeked of booze, and the kids at school called him Mr. Mock because he was such a fraud.

Sue went along with the charade that she was actually learning something since it beat going to school. After each lesson, Danny and I imitated him in an attempt to get a cheap laugh out of our heartbroken sister. She was usually too distracted and sad to appreciate the brilliance in our humor. That didn't stop us, we still tried to cheer her up.

My grandma had flown to Ohio to handle the dirty deed. She agreed to deliver Sue's baby to the eager couple in St. Petersburg. This would also give Grandma a chance to meet the parents and build a bond with them. She had already agreed to act as Sue's spy and keep her apprised of her daughter's upbringing.

Sue went into labor on the last day of November, a frosty Wednesday morning. The winds were over twenty miles per hour, the temperature never reached forty degrees that day. I found it amusing that Sue's water broke on the flowery, velveteen couch. The second innocent sofa drenched by my sister.

Grandma called the doctor when Sue ran to the bathroom screaming and locked the door. Grandma Alice had five kids, she knew when it was time to drop a baby. Sue holed up in the bathroom in a panic. She was also anxious because her time with the baby was coming to an end.

Grandma tried her best to answer the physician's questions, but he insisted on speaking with the woman in labor. Sue finally emerged from the safety of the bathroom. Reluctantly, she responded to the doctor's questions. When he heard that her water had broken, he ordered her to the hospital immediately. She was about to have her baby.

Sue started to push, things weren't going well. Her hips were not broad enough to accommodate the seven-pound-three-ounce baby exiting her young body. A doctor ran from the room and returned, wheeling a metal tank. He placed a mask over Sue's nose and mouth and within seconds, she was unconscious.

Exiting the birth canal, the obstetrician declared an emergency cesarean section when the baby's neck started to bend. The scar would act as another reminder of what she lost, as well as a badge of honor for the sacrifices she made for her baby.

On the cold winter evening of November 30, 1983, at 10:19 p.m., Sue's beautiful baby girl was born. Before her new parents named her Rebecca, the nurses affectionately called her "Baby Gossage." Rebecca was perfect. She had brown hair and long delicate fingers. Sue was allowed to feed her a bottle and snuggle her. She whispered her love and admiration to the child she so desperately wanted to keep.

Danny, Jimmy, and I urged Mom to bring us to meet Sue's baby. Because of the consequences to our young psyches, Mom debated. She knew it was hard enough for us without meeting her.

After Amy was born, we became so enamored with babies. We could not believe Sue's was never coming home. Especially Danny and Jimmy. The boys had a soft spot for Amy. They relished the idea of having yet another little one running around Kimmensville. Again, Mom sadly explained that that was not going to be the case with this little girl. A lovely family in Florida was anxiously waiting for her.

Mom caved in and drove us to the hospital during visiting hours. We walked through the elevator doors and down the linoleum hallway. Nurses hustled past us with clipboards. Silently, we followed the signs pointing to the Maternity Ward.

We paused when we saw a rectangular window revealing rows of baby bassinets. Nervous and full of curiosity, we clutched the windowsill with our fingertips and stood on our tippy toes. The squirming infants were swaddled in pink and blue blankets. A bassinet holding a little, pink bundle labeled, "Baby Gossage" sat in the middle row.

The love that Danny and I felt towards Sue and Rebecca that day was overwhelming. We laughed and cried at the same time, our feelings so jumbled. We were incredibly proud of our big sister for standing up to the obstacles she had faced as a pregnant teen. She had made this beautiful, healthy person.

At the same time, we knew the baby was leaving, and that was crushing us. We stayed there as long as we could, then sadly walked to the car and drove home. Sniffling, we passed up Mom's offer to stop for a treat.

The next day, Sue was asked to make her final decision as Rebecca's parent. Did she want to list the father's name on the hospital birth certificate? She asked for more time.

My best friend, Dawn, was close with his twin. She felt compelled to call Mark and tell him what a mistake he was making. She asked him to reconsider walking away from his beautiful daughter. At first, he tried to justify his decision. Pointing out his parent's wishes, school, his job, blah, blah, blah. Dawn badgered Mark until he finally agreed to visit Sue and the baby.

Hoping for privacy, she asked Mom to stay home that night. Sue fixed her hair without a mirror and waited. She was hopeful that she wouldn't have to go through with the adoption.

Mark never showed up. After crying herself to sleep, Sue held her head high when the nurse entered her room the next morning and repeated the question about the birth certificate. "List the father as unknown," my sister answered.

In an attempt to quell her nerves, Mom had left to go shopping. She returned with Rebecca's first outfit, a pink dress with matching hat and booties. Mom wanted her granddaughter to look her best. As she snapped pictures of Sue and her baby, our mom hoped and prayed that she would once again see her grandchild. Sue used those few photographs to start a scrapbook of memories.

That weekend, after spending five days with her baby girl, Sue was wheeled out of the hospital. She held Rebecca against her chest until the last possible moment. The harsh realization hit her: this was the moment she had been dreading the most. Sue reluctantly handed her daughter to Grandma and watched them drive away. Her baby ripped a piece of her heart out and took it with her that day.

My grandma boarded an airplane at the Akron/Canton Airport with Rebecca. The baby was swaddled in several layers of blankets that were shed when they landed in the Sunshine State. They left so much more behind than the cold weather that day.

Six months later, I browsed the Mother's Day cards at Baltzly Drug store looking for the perfect message for my mom. As I was perusing the rack, a card resonated with me. A beautiful vase of flowers adorned the front with a lovely sentiment inside about bringing a child into the world. Sue had given birth and survived the most challenging year of her life, but she was not able to celebrate Mother's Day. It didn't seem fair. I bought two cards that year and walked to the counter with a lump in my throat.

Unfortunately, the card did not come across as I had intended. Sue thought it was rather mean to remind her that she was technically a mother, but had no reason to celebrate the holiday. I felt terrible that my motive had come across as so cruel.

I was actually trying to tell her how proud of her I was for everything she had done. I believed she should be able to celebrate this day. Her child was alive because of her. But we weren't good at expressing our feelings unless it was to yell at each other. I started to explain, but she ran out of our bedroom and locked herself in the bathroom to cry. I let it go and hoped she would, as well.

Grandma had turned out to be an awesome secret agent. Every Sunday, she saw the Kuruc family at church. Grandma also discovered they never called her Rebecca. She was Becky from the start.

Initially, Kathy did not feel threatened by sweet, old Grandma Alice. She allowed her to give Becky birthday and Christmas cards, a crisp five or ten-dollar bill always tucked inside along with her loopy greeting, "*Love, Alice Black xoxo.*" If Grandma had her camera, which happened to be quite often, Kathy allowed her to snap pictures of Becky that she sent to Sue.

For years, my young niece was suspicious of the mystery lady that paid so much attention to her at church. She never said anything to her parents, but she thought it was a little creepy. She smiled sheepishly and accepted whatever the old lady had for her.

Kathy occasionally slipped photographs into Grandma's hand as they parted ways. Grandma would rush home to call Sue and tell her another picture of Becky was on the way. She described the photo, so Sue had something to look forward to. Often ending with, "Becky looks so much like you."

My sister decorated a store-bought photo album with fabric and lace. She carefully placed all the mementos of her daughter, beginning with her pregnancy and Becky's first five days in Ohio. Pictures her daughter would never find in her own baby book. The album grew, Grandma continued to send photos, and Sue shed tears as she added them.

In 1985, I met my niece in Florida as a rambunctious two-year-old. Kathy coached her to say, "Hi, Aunt Lisa." I melted and wanted to hug her all afternoon, but I couldn't catch her. I assumed this interaction would be the norm as she grew up, it was the last time I saw her as a child.

Fear and uncertainty had set in. Kathy started to distance herself and wasn't as friendly to her old pal. Grandma got an occasional wave from Kathy and a smile from Becky, she knew she was being shunned. She respected their wishes. The smuggled pictures ended as abruptly as Grandma's stories about the latest Becky sighting.

Our lost girl did have a few shining stars in her life. Her babysitter, Elsie D'Amico, was one of the brightest and shiniest of all. After Becky arrived from the cold northeast, she immediately bonded with Elsie who became a second mother to her. Through example, Becky was taught hard work, love, and respect. Over the decades, Elsie cared for hundreds of kids in her home daycare center. At a young age, Becky played the role of caretaker herself, always pitching in to assist with the younger children.

Her adopted dad, Ron, was also a bright spot in her life. His light blue eyes twinkled each time he looked at his little girl. He gave her everything she needed, especially his love and admiration. They quickly bonded, and she became Daddy's Little Girl.

Ron was such an excellent replacement to the boy that could have raised her. This is why Sue could have no regrets. Her intentions had been to give her child a life that she could not provide. A father that looked at Becky with a sparkle in his eye and called her "Princess" was something that Sue wanted to provide her daughter, but she never could have promised that.

Kathy was a busy working mom and already had a special connection with Becky's big brother. At a young age, Keith required quite a bit of attention and was treated for various behavioral issues. Prescription medicine soon followed. He was spiraling out of control, requiring more attention from Kathy. Becky's bond with Elsie and Ron had grown stronger.

When Becky was fourteen, we received news about her family. Becky's parents had split up, and her mom moved back home to Missouri. The grim financial situation had forced her dad to sell their house.

Ron stayed with a friend until he got back on his feet while Becky lived with Elsie and her husband, Papa Moe. Keith had turned to drugs and alcohol and wasn't listening to anyone's advice. His wise sister used to keep him on track and give him money and guidance when he needed it most. There was nothing left she could do.

Becky and Keith were unaware they were adopted. Elsie and her family were asked to keep this information private. Which they did until their grandson thought she needed to hear the truth.

Rickie grew up with Becky and was like a brother. After her parents had split, she felt so lonely. He told Becky what she most needed to hear. There was a huge family in Ohio and Florida that cared about her more than she could ever know. He stressed that we were respecting Kathy and Ron's wishes, but we had never left her side.

Rickie continued to spill the beans. Her young birth mother had been collecting photos and patiently waiting to meet her. When Becky heard that she had two half-brothers, she couldn't contain her excitement. She longed to meet the family she later compared to a "Jerry Springer Show." Almost fifty relatives all over the country she could call her own. When my niece discovered that her great-grandma lived nearby, she desperately wanted to visit her. Now it was her turn to be patient.

Becky felt the love in her heart for her birth mother and knew one day she would meet her. Rickie was relieved. At the same time, he was afraid his own family would never see her again if Ron and Kathy found out. Becky was special to the entire D'Amico clan, and they could not risk the chance of never seeing her again. Her friend didn't want to ask her to keep such a big secret, but he knew Becky needed to hear about us. She promised to keep this incredible news to herself.

When Becky was a freshman in high school, less than a year after finding out the truth, her adopted mother died. The news hit our circle, we were stunned--a heart attack at any age is tragic. We soon learned that Kathy had fibbed to us about her age. She had been worried we would never grant her wish if we

167

knew the truth. She was actually in her fifties when she adopted Becky.

Becky loved her dad and was grateful she still had him, but she felt sad going through life without a mother. Her emotions and curiosity were raging. She had to see Alice Black again, it was too important for a phone call. My niece sat down with Elsie and told her that she knew everything. Then she begged for her great-grandmother's address.

Elsie reassured Becky that someone from Sue's family was always watching out for her. Great-grandma Alice kept an eye on her at church. The nurse colleague of Kathy's she met a few times was her great-aunt Nancy. And by pure coincidence, the principal at her school was our cousin Bobby's wife.

She planned to ask Grandma all the questions that were swirling through her mind. Elsie had recovered from the fact she kept this information to herself for a year and told Rickie's dad to drive her. For the first time, Becky would meet our beautiful matriarch as her great-grandmother.

Grandma was sitting in her condo watching a *Rockford Files* rerun, starring her favorite movie star, James Garner. When she heard a knock on her door, she assumed it was a neighbor dropping off a recipe or a newspaper clipping. She was shocked to see her first-born great-granddaughter on her porch.

Becky's long legs were shaking with anticipation. How would her family react to her finally being a part of their lives? When Grandma opened the door, Becky blurted out, "*I know who you are! I know you're my great-grandma, and I want to meet my family!*"

Thank goodness Grandma had a healthy heart. Her fingers flew to her face as tears welled up in her blue eyes. She reached out to hug Becky and pulled her into her home, followed by her sniffling escort.

168

Grandma led them to her sofa in the front room, squeezing Becky's hand. She gasped a few times and said in her sweet, sing-songy voice, "Becky!! I can't believe it's *you*. I can't believe you're *here*." She offered them a drink, "Coffee, pop, beer?" They both politely declined and sat on the couch, big smiles on their faces.

Grandma jumped up and grabbed some photo albums, then squeezed between Becky and John on the sofa. They flipped through the pages, looking at pictures of everyone that longed to meet her.

Becky cried when she saw our big family. The resemblances were uncanny. Not only to her birth mother but Amy. If they were a few years closer, she and Amy could have been mistaken for twins. Grandma flipped through the crackly pages of the photo albums.

Then, she asked Becky if she wanted to call her mom in Ohio. Becky absolutely wanted to talk to Sue. She had waited over a year for this moment. Grandma, quick on her feet for an eighty-two-year-old, leaped from her chair. She opened the address book tucked under the phone and punched in Sue's phone number.

My big sister answered the phone and heard the words she had longed for since she was a teenager. "Hi, Mom! It's your daughter, Becky!" It took a moment for it to sink in. Tears welled in her eyes. "I'm at Great-grandma Alice's house, and I know about everything. I know who you are, I want to meet you." Sue's dream finally came true, and she broke down.

When I answered the phone that evening and heard Becky on the other end, I thought I was hallucinating. She was so excited, we laughed and cried at the same time. I echoed what she had just heard from her mom, that we all loved her and could not wait to meet her.

I called Sue right away and offered her an airline ticket. She was six-months pregnant with her fourth child, she never hesitated. Sue packed her bags while I made the arrangements. It was Labor Day weekend, and Amy happened to be going to Florida the next day for vacation. I booked Sue on the same flight so they could travel together, both nervous and thrilled to meet Becky.

My niece not only looked like Amy, but she also sounded like her. When they answered the phone or had their backs turned, it was hard to pick them out. They took pictures of Becky's feet alongside their own. Her second toe longer than the big toe, a family trait passed down to the girls. They shared family stories and snapped pictures of each other. Everyone in such high spirits, they barely slept that night.

It was 1998 when they finally met. Sue was with Kevin now, and they were expecting their first child together, her third son. She shared with Becky that they decided to name the baby Danny. She told Becky all about our little brother and how he had cried when he had to say goodbye to her. Becky would have loved Danny. He would have spoiled her rotten.

It was so upsetting for Sue to leave her for a second time. They agreed to keep in touch and planned Becky's first visit to Ohio. Sue backed out of the driveway to leave for the airport, another piece of her heart missing. She finally had found her daughter, and now she had to leave again. Becky's life was in Florida with her dad, Elsie, and the friends she grew up with. Sue understood this, just like Becky knew her mom couldn't pick up and move her life south.

The summer of 1999, Becky visited Ohio and met her brothers, including her new baby brother, Danny. She instantly fit into our crazy family.

170

Two years later, Sue's wedding to Kevin was complete when Becky stood proudly by her side. She was stunning in a bright red, satin dress, next to her three handsome brothers. It was perfect in every way. They even held the ceremony in the church that sat on the edge of the Elms Golf Course.

Ten years after Sue's wedding and thirteen years after we reunited with my niece, the entire Ohio clan trekked south for Becky's wedding. We booked adjoining rooms at a hotel in downtown St. Petersburg and partied joyously every night. We were so grateful and proud to represent the bride. As we watched her dad walk her down the aisle, a river of tears flowed.

It was one of the happiest days of Sue's life. She was never going to be the parent that raised her, but she had been the one to give Becky life. She is forever her mom and not a day passes without Sue thinking of her.

Even my father made amends with his first grandchild when he whispered an apology in her ear as they danced at her wedding. She didn't have to look at Grandpa Steve to know he was also silently crying.

There are many regrets about not having Becky in our lives for her first fifteen years. But, because of her upbringing, she is the independent and successful woman she is today, fortunate to have such influential role models in her life. Sue had always wanted her daughter to have an incredible life. And because of her strength and love, she did.

Daniel, My Brother

At the end of the long, dismal hallway was the ICU. Mom, Dad, Sue, and I were dreading what we were about to witness. It was a large area with curtains bordering the individual rooms and intermittent beeps echoing from the various medical devices that were keeping the patients alive. My body shivered as if it was February and not the middle of July. Dad slowly parted the baby blue curtains and the four of us, tear-filled, frightened, and hanging onto each other, slowly entered the room.

There he was, covered from the waist down by a white hospital sheet and bare chest that bore two circular patches with cords attached leading to a machine which monitored his heartbeat. It was strong. The doctors had wrapped Danny's swollen skull in a gauze bandage. The dressing ended right above his puffy, closed eyes.

He was breathing slowly with the assistance of a noisy respirator, his chest rising and falling with each single breath. We could not control our sobs, as each of us touched his arms and held his hands, reassuring him how much we loved him, begging and pleading to please hang in there and pull through.

Mom had already called her family to deliver the tragic news. Her two sisters, Nancy and Judi, would both fly in the next afternoon. Nancy was still living in Florida with her family and Judi had recently moved to California. I wasn't surprised they were coming.

Nancy was a nurse and was always there to assist with family medical catastrophes; not to mention, she loved us. Aunt Judi always had a special bond with all of Betty's kids from the time we lived next door to her. She had no sons and adored Danny as if he was her own.

We continued to talk to Danny, though we weren't sure he could hear us. Our hopes dwindled as the hours pressed on with no sign of improvement. Mom held Danny's hand, as we all stood around his bed, and announced that Aunt Judi was coming to see him.

At that exact moment, his arm bent at the elbow, and his left forearm shot straight up in the air. The monitors peaked showing an increased heart rate. Our expectations were high as we yelled to alert the nurse of his progress.

The RN diminished this newfound hope by stating it was common and was just a muscle reflex, not a sign from a medical perspective that he actually heard the good news. We protested that the reaction was clearly at the same time we told him his beloved aunt was coming to see him and the coincidence was just too great. She sadly shook her head and said she was sorry, but that a patient in this condition was probably not going to hear us.

We didn't care what she said and continued to reassure him of our love, asked him to stay with us, prayed for him, and recalled the time spent with our little man.

We kept on all through the night, until we were asked to let him rest. A kind ICU nurse suggested we do the same and led us to a family waiting room, designed for evenings such as this, with long couches to sleep on.

Monday morning, we were awakened by someone from the medical staff who informed us that the neurosurgeon would like to meet with all four of us. We sat impatiently, the events from the night before flooding our minds. We still couldn't believe this nightmare, so horrible it didn't seem real. Our small reprieve from reality during our slumber was over, we had to face the truth.

The MD assigned to my brother's care had believed Sue and I were old enough to hear the condition of our brother and to

173

be a part of the decision-making process. I asked myself, *What decision-making process?* My stomach churned. I was not attached to my body any longer and watched the scene unfold as a bystander.

The results of tests and MRIs, the doctor continued, as well as other medical evidence, concluded that Danny was brain dead. His heart is healthy, he's a tough young man, the doctor added, trying to soften the blow. Yes, we know that, he's *fourteen*.

"What does it mean if he survives this ordeal?" my mom asked through her shivers and tears. "It means he won't ever walk, talk, or be able to take care of himself, with no chance of improvement. The bullet passed through his brain, there was just too much damage. He would be bound to a wheelchair with breathing tubes and would need constant care and attention," the doctor bluntly and honestly answered.

He would not continue to enjoy the life of a teenager who could play sports, dance, laugh, and talk with his friends. He would never fall in love and have a family of his own.

Hearing this stark prognosis, I knew instantly: this was not the way Danny would want to live. He did this for a reason we would never truly know. But to save him now at this point, to make a choice as to whether he lives out his life in this confinement, and without being able to ask him what he wanted, was a huge burden for all of us.

After the doctor had delivered all of the medical information, he left us with two options. Insert a permanent breathing tube to prolong Danny's life in a vegetative state, or disconnect the tubes and let him live on his own as long as he was able. The doctor exited the room to let us talk in private. Each of us knew what we had to do, but it was not easy for any of us to admit it.

We held each other and cried, no one wanted to say or hear the words. Sue and I finally reassured our aching parents that Danny would never want to live an isolated life with permanent brain damage. They agreed with us, but it didn't make it any easier when we later told the doctor our decision--unhook the breathing tubes and let our little boy go peacefully.

Having been raised to believe you should always help others, my mother insisted on organ donation. Danny's eyesight was perfect, his heart was healthy, and his kidneys were untarnished. Mom still has the thank you cards from each of the organ beneficiaries, with the bottom cut off by the donation center to conceal their identity.

Waiting for a perfect match for his heart allowed us to steal more time by his bedside as we tried to stretch every minute. Friends and family rotated in and out of the hospital waiting room for the next two days.

Our small community pulled together and gave us the strength to keep going. Prayer chains at church were being held, casseroles were being baked, and sympathy cards were being purchased all over town for the Gossage family's imminent loss.

We stood vigil by his side and never left the hospital for more than a few hours each, and never at the same time, just in case Danny needed us. Amy stayed at my uncle's house next door, the remaining family members spent two more nights at the hospital grieving and praying for a miracle. Sue and I drove home for a change of clothes, and so she could replay the details of what happened that evening.

I didn't want to see the aftermath, but the urge to know was too powerful. I felt a chill when I opened, slowly, Danny's bedroom door. I flipped on the light and immediately saw the dark stain on his goldenrod rug. This is where Sue found him after she heard the gunshot. Dad had shot skeets across the street enough times that she knew deep in her heart, the loud noise in the house was not something falling to the ground, as she had hoped.

Sue knew he'd been upset that evening, but never could have expected the scene she would walk into. I stood in the doorway and tried to imagine what my sister had experienced that night.

The only evidence was on his bedroom rug and crudely covered up in the basement. Sue was doing laundry in the cellar when she noticed the graffiti on the den wall that divided our basement, allowing our father a private hideaway when he wanted to be alone, which was quite often. The only message my brother left was painted in six-foot letters across the outside wall of my dad's den with black spray paint. Dad's friend attempted to cover the scrawl to protect his feelings, I could still make out the word PRICK.

Sue had dropped the basket and ran upstairs to confront our brother and find out what he was thinking. She heard loud music blaring from his room and found his door handle was jammed. The bathroom was the only interior door that had a lock for privacy, so we used my old crutches as an alternative.

Sue was only able to budge the crutch a bit and yelled through the small opening in the door, "Danny! What are you doing? Dad is going to kill you when he gets home. Why did you write that?" Of course, she didn't mean that literally, it's a phrase some throw around way too casually.

A few moments later, Danny released the barricade and cracked the door, peering out at her with wild eyes. She noticed sweat dripping down his face, and he was very agitated. He didn't bother to turn down the volume of the music as he pleaded with her, "How do I get it off?"

Sue said she wasn't sure because he sprayed the paint directly on the wooden wall, she suggested he try gasoline. They searched the garage until he found the can we used for the lawn mower. Danny was evidently having regrets and ran downstairs with the canister and rag where he attempted to scrub off his profanity.

Unfortunately, as hard as they rubbed, it did not remove the stain. *"I don't care anymore!!"* he screamed as he ran upstairs. Sue followed and heard him slam his bedroom door shut before replacing the crutch. She shook her head and felt sorry for him. She wasn't sure how to help her little brother out of this situation.

No more than ten minutes later, Sue heard the gunshot from behind his closed door. She tried to turn the knob, then banged with her fists when she found it blocked again. The same haunting song he had played earlier, *When Doves Cry*, was wafting from his room.

Sue threw her body against the door repeatedly until she felt the crutch begin to slip. The fear of losing Danny was giving her the courage and strength to continue to slam the door with her shoulder. She had to save her little brother. She was the only one home and his only hope.

Sue ran to the front of the house and attempted to gain entry through his bedroom window, it was too high for her. She ran back into the house and continued to ram the door until it finally sprung free.

Danny had turned off the lights. Sue instantly smelled the gun powder. She flipped the switch. While Prince continued to sing, Danny lay on the floor bleeding to death, a .32 caliber nearby.

Sue rushed to the dining room wild with fear. She panicked and called her boyfriend, who in turn called 9-1-1. Chris reached our house at eight thirty, almost the exact same time as the ambulance. This strangely coincided with our dinner at Wendy's, when I thought I had heard a siren.

Uncle Jim ran from next door when he saw the commotion of the ambulance and jumped in the back to ride along with Danny to the emergency room. Sue and Chris called our parents at the Merriman's to deliver the harrowing news before they drove to Dawn's house in an attempt to find me.

As I stood frozen in Danny's bedroom doorway, I was amazed at how brave Sue and Chris had been to have handled this disaster on their own. I am not sure I would be holding up as well if I was the sister to find our dying brother.

I cautiously looked around his room to get a sense of his final thoughts and actions. We would not find the sketches he hid behind his dresser for months, but I noticed Mandy's second-grade school photo was still tacked to his bulletin board.

The bubbly blonde was his best friend in elementary school until she succumbed to the impact of a sedan one afternoon while crossing the street to check the mail. Although he'd been as heartbroken as her own family, gentle soul that Danny was, he agreed to give the eulogy at her funeral.

I opened his closet door. Draped on a hanger was the graffiti shirt he was wearing before I left the house that fateful evening. Tears streamed down my face when I realized he changed clothes so I could wear it, which is exactly what my thoughtful, kind-hearted brother would have done for one of his sisters.

I returned to the hospital in worse shape than when I left, realizing I had changed. I felt older and more scared about my future than I had ever been. A short week ago I was at the movies with my friends, laughing at the antics of Bill Murray and Harold Ramis in *Ghostbusters*. I felt as if I had aged a decade in a week. I think that's why I responded the way I did in the hospital cafeteria when Dad invited Sue and me to join him for a talk.

After choosing wobbly Jello and pop, we selected a table in the corner away from everyone. Sue and I picked at our food and sipped our drinks. Dad stared at the ground, legs spread apart, hands folded, and elbows resting on his knees to support himself. He seemed to be in a sad trance, most likely practicing what he was about to say to his remaining teenagers. His eyes were red and watery like I had never seen them before. He finally looked up and said he was sorry. He was sorry he wasn't a better father, that he wasn't around much.

As a kid, I was the most accepting of Dad and his hobbies and tagged along on a few outings. He just didn't know how to show affection towards his children. As much as I wanted a fresh start with him and wanted to believe his words, it was too soon.

I knew deep in my heart that none of us could have known that Danny was this sad, angry, and depressed. He and Dad didn't always see eye to eye, and my only brother was the protector of his girls. But, no one expected this.

I spoke first. "I'm sorry Dad, but I'm sixteen and Sue's eighteen. We don't need a father as much as we did when we were younger. We needed you then, not now. I'm sorry, but you're too late." Sue nodded her head in agreement, then lowered her shoulders, and cried into her hands. Dad slumped into his lap, covered his face, and cried like a baby. I was as stoic as I could be but was only a child myself, so eventually, I sank in my chair and cried along with them.

My parents gave me a Valium that third and final night at the hospital, I needed to rest. I slept so deeply I almost missed the last rights Fr. Daum gave to my brother. They said they couldn't wake me and I believed them--I was a hard person to wake up without a sedative in my system. But something caused me to sit straight up around 3:50 a.m. I found myself alone in the family waiting room.

179

After I had realized where I was, I knew they must be with Danny and rushed out the door, around the corner to the ICU. When I gradually parted the curtains and peeked in, I saw my family standing, hand in hand with their heads hung low surrounding Danny's bed, the priest blessing my brother, and making the sign of the cross over his forehead.

This meant the hospital had found a beneficiary for my brother's heart and would unplug his respirator today. I joined the prayer circle, and we all sobbed as we said our final goodbyes to Danny.

Sue and I knew exactly what Dan would want to wear for his final appearance: the black and white outfit he wore to the eighth-grade Valentine's dance where he was voted first runner-up to the Valentine's King.

I recalled, as we solemnly laid out his parachute pants and ironed his white tuxedo shirt, that we shared our disappointment with Danny that he wasn't selected as King. We knew from the number of girls that called him every evening that he was one of the most popular boys in his junior high. Danny laughed and said not to feel sorry for him, he was happy with his spot in the lineup because the King had to wear a crown all night that resembled the Imperial Margarine commercials in the '70s.

Then he did his imitation of the little boy singing, "*Yes I am the muffin man…*" licking the margarine from his fingers as a crown appeared on his head.

As I drove to the shoe store to buy heels, I recalled how Danny could always make us laugh with his imitations, his playful sense of humor, and the funny songs he created out of just noises. No longer would I sit on the couch and watch *Benny Hill* and chuckle at the innuendoes and parodies with my little sidekick. I was going to miss so many things about him.

180

Shopping for such a sad event was too much for me, I rushed home in hysterics after buying the first pair of white heels the clerk presented.

I was enrolled at a business school my upcoming junior year. My new clothes that summer included office attire, which was the protocol for the Steno Word Processing students at R.G. Drage. After my shopping spree, I did a runway show down the hall and into the living room where Danny sat to admire his big sister.

He especially loved the aqua blue circle dress I had picked out with a white, patent leather belt and buttons mimicking the trends of the fifties—the dress I chose to wear for his memorial because I knew Danny would have liked it. I also think he would have agreed the white pumps matched perfectly.

Almost five hundred people attended the calling hours for Danny at Paquelet Funeral Home, where my grandfather Howard's service was held fifteen years prior. Danny looked so peaceful in his casket, wearing black parachute pants and jacket with his skinny, leather tie lying gently across the pleats of his white shirt. Mom asked that four single red roses be placed in his folded hands; one from each of his girls.

The immediate family lined up to greet the visitors. I looked up and saw Miss Dietz at the front of the line, red-faced and crying with Danny's friends from school, and the neighborhood families behind her. I wasn't sure how I was going to hold myself together.

Six-year-old Amy appeared to be more stable than all of us. She was finally allowed to see her brother, one last time. She struggled to understand why her family was so sad and why Danny wasn't moving. Normally the center of attention, Amy was now in the shadow. Her life was suddenly ominous. She would tell me later, she felt abandoned.

We all knew how much she loved her big brother and what a guardian he was of our youngest sibling. Amy was now protecting him by standing watch on the prayer bench directly in front of the casket. Our baby sister leaned in to block the outreached hands and leaning faces that were trying to give him one last touch or kiss. Both calling hour sessions lasted two hours each and Amy never left her post.

The next afternoon, St. Barbara's church was packed with people from all over the Massillon area. Our family unanimously agreed on the six pallbearers who would carefully carry Danny's casket down the aisle and into the hearse.

At the head of the pack was Jimmy, of course, and Kandi, another best friend and confidant who was often mistaken for his sister. It was not only the physical resemblance, but they were also inseparable as children, often requesting each other when given a chance to choose a friend to come over for the afternoon.

We laid Danny to rest on a Friday, in the plot next to our grandfather Howard Black, and cousin Kathleen Black who died shortly after her premature birth. This left one final spot open for almost thirty years before Grandmother Alice joined them at the St. Barbara's Cemetery.

The Black family plot is maintained and regularly visited by various people, mostly by my mom. Dawn, Nancy, Sue, and I placed my bouquet of flowers from Karlene's wedding the day Danny would have turned fifteen. Sue and I decorated a tree for his grave our first Christmas without him. And every July eighteenth, Dad never neglects to visit his only son. Mom thoughtfully plants flowers on holidays and plucks the weeds regularly, keeping the plot tidy.

Although we always remember Danny at every family gathering and holiday, there remains an empty feeling in the room. We miss his smile, his laughter. We miss his unique presence.

That's the way it felt at Uncle Jim's home following the funeral. So many people filed in and out of the split-level house, bringing casseroles and condolence cards. Danny wasn't there to make us laugh about the casseroles that lingered in our freezer months later, he would have had a joke or two about them.

My mind was foggy. I didn't listen to what everyone was saying to me and can't recall all of their names. That afternoon in Kimmensville, I do know we were surrounded by an abundance of sorrow, and of love.

Chris, Sue, and I drove Aunt Judi to the airport the next morning, and as I hugged her, I promised to see her in nine days when I joined them in Carlsbad, California for the summer. I didn't want to be home right now with my feelings still so raw and painful. Things would never be the same again. I thought a summer on the beach was what I needed.

As it turned out, I fell in love with California. I just wished Danny was there to join me, I know he would have enjoyed boogie boarding and hanging out with Aunt Judi.

She taught me how to drive a stick shift so I could drop her off at work and use her car. I'd hang out at the beach and boogie board in the Pacific, or I'd shop all day. Aunt Judi taught me how to cook. I hosted her spirited friends after Uncle Jim taught me how to make Kamikazes. I forgot about my own life for a little while.

We took their dogs to the beach and ate hors d'oeuvre as we watched the sunset. We visited Hollywood and took my picture on Sunset Blvd, not far from the purple lingerie store, Frederick's of Hollywood.

One night, we dressed up and saw a play, then stopped for dessert on the way home at the Häagen-Dazs ice cream store, which was shaped like a soft serve cone. I never wanted to leave and knew I would be back. I was convinced Danny would have loved it.

I thought of him every day and all of the things he was missing and would never experience. That's when I vowed to live my life to the fullest, knowing Danny couldn't. And I promised him that when I experienced something new, I would do it for both of us. It filled a void to think of him as if he was actually there and not just in my heart.

My vacation in California ended, and I returned to discover that my mother was divorcing her husband after almost twenty years of marriage. Dad moved his things out while I was gone and rented an apartment in Orrville, near the patrol where he was stationed.

Dad remarried two years later, and Carol would become our stepmother. There have been no hard feelings. My two moms get along great and we all agree my parents should have divorced many years earlier, or maybe they never should have married in the first place. I am glad they did, though, because I have my beautiful, strong sisters. And I have my memories of our funny and compassionate brother.

Life A.D.

Life after Danny was excruciating. His death affected each of us differently, coping in our unique ways. Nothing was ever the same again for so many people. Sadly, some of his friends said that he had mentioned suicide, but they thought he was kidding. It was something kids joked about, not something that was carried out. Or so they thought.

Later, we learned just how much he talked about it. He had made a pact with a friend; they both planned to kill themselves that evening. Fortunately for his ally's family, he didn't go through with it, but I imagine the toll it took on him was immense.

Hours before, Danny called a girl he liked and told her "goodbye." She thought he was acting strange, but never fathomed the news she received the next morning. Word spread throughout town like a wildfire.

I have asked myself countless times, "What if I had stopped the car and asked Danny why he was acting like it was the last time he would ever see me? Would he have answered me?" Sue also berates herself for not handling the evening differently, "Why didn't I just grab a can of paint and help him cover the damn obscenity?" Mom was puzzled--how did she miss the clues? It was her precious son! For months, Dad sat at his office desk and aimlessly stared out of the window.

We all blamed ourselves, contemplating ways we each could have prevented his suicide. Like losing a leg or arm and still feeling the mystery limb, we reached for him and expected him to be there. Disappointed time and time again.

Mom's life as Mother Goose abruptly changed. While raising us, she never held more than a part-time job. Her college education equated to one semester of Speech and Hearing

185

Therapy classes at Kent State University. Then she found out she was pregnant with Sue. Nineteen years later, Mom was the head of our household. She had to provide for us and supplement our meager child support.

The first big decision Mom, Sue, and I made together was to move. We could not live in a home filled with signs of Danny's violent death. We sold our house on the golf course to our neighbors, Bev and Gene. Of course, they had mixed feelings, but Bev dreamed of living next to her grandchildren. So, they remodeled it for Karlene and her fiancé.

Less than two months after burying our brother, Amy began her education. Stoically carrying her Care Bears lunch box, Mom held her hand and walked her to the first-grade classroom at Tuslaw Elementary. I had started my junior year at R.G. Drage Technical High School where Sue was finishing her senior year. College was not in our future. Survival was now the topic at the dinner table.

Mom found a job as a nursing assistant at a retirement center. Sacrificing her evenings so we could drive her car to school, she agreed to the night shift. We promised to take care of Amy, and we always did.

Staying in Massillon became harder. We tried, but the reminders were too painful. Mom decided that at the end of the school year, we would move to Florida. Trying to save the little money she made from the sale of the house for our relocation, we looked for temporary housing in our rural school district.

We searched for weeks and couldn't find a rental. Desperate, Mom bought an awful, double-wide trailer on a big lot about a mile from our home. We were naive dog owners. Mom assumed a good carpet cleaning would eliminate the odor of cat that overpowered us. It was a painful ten months.

That winter, the wind blew through the cracks in the mobile home and chilled our bones. We tried to avoid the frigid walls as we slept, the thin insulation provided little protection from the harsh weather. I discovered the crevices allowed more than gusts of wind into our aluminum house the night a gray field mouse scurried across my face.

I felt the furry rodent on my cheek, bolted upright, dislodged its grip, and tossed him. He had landed on my pillow and dashed between my mattress and the wall. I jumped out of bed and did the heebie-jeebie jig around my bedroom, waking my sister. "What the *hell* are you doing?!" For weeks, I slept in a hoodie. I cinched the string so that only my nose was visible from the tiny opening.

We all did our best to support each other. Sue and I chose to bury our sorrow, each of us refusing to see a counselor or join Mom and Amy at a Compassionate Friends gathering. We were not up for sharing our thoughts and feelings with other survivors. And we were *not* going to talk to Father Daum or Dr. Marisigan. We insisted we were fine.

Sue got a job at Laid Back Records in downtown Massillon where they sold music, T-shirts, concert tickets, waterbeds, and bongs. Most nights Sue and I went out to escape our pain, as well as the smell of the cat spray. In place of therapy, we kept ourselves preoccupied with throwing and attending parties.

We had plenty of music and booze at our first bash at the trailer, but we didn't account for the parking. Cars lined both sides of our narrow, unlit road making it impossible for more than one car to pass at a time.

Late that night, a drunk driver had barreled down the dark street. He hit a parked car, ricocheted, and hit the second one before settling on the hood of a third vehicle.

The music was so loud that no one had heard the impact of the crash. At some point in the evening, a drunken girl came stumbling into our living room. She was babbling about a dead man in our front yard. Before she stumbled away, I heard her say, "*I cub-bered him up with a blanket.*"

Doubtful, I ran to the front yard. A big lump was lying near my driveway, covered by Amy's fleece blanket. I lifted a corner, exposing a bloodied man and screamed, "*Call 9-1-1!!*"

My sister and I told everyone to leave the trailer immediately. We handed out bags of empty beer bottles and asked our guests to toss them on their way home. Before the cops arrived, most of the underage kids had scrambled. Only the owners of the wrecked vehicles stayed behind.

The ambulance sped away with the injured drunk, and we sobered up enough to give statements to the police officers. As the smashed cars were towed away, our perplexed mother approached the driveway, police still obstructing the entrance.

For some reason, Sue and I thought it was a good idea to have another party the following weekend. Our rationale was that Amy was going to Dad's house again, so why not.

There were no car accidents this time, but a fight between two guys took out the awning on our front porch. That was harder to explain. We didn't want to admit to hosting another unauthorized drinking spree for our underage friends. Mom had enough on her mind, as long as we were safe, she didn't get upset about much of anything.

Sue's boyfriend moved away to attend his freshman year of college in Texas on a baseball scholarship. Committed to their long-distance relationship, they racked up costly phone bills.

Chris only returned once that year for winter break, that was enough. The following spring, Sue recognized the familiar signs of pregnancy and called Chris with the news.

They had started dating after she lost Becky. Chris understood the fear in her voice. He promised there was no way in hell he would allow her to go through more heartbreak and loss. The good man insisted on dropping out of college and moved home to support my big sister and his first child.

Sue sadly announced to Mom, Amy, and me that she would not be moving to Florida with us that summer. Chris proposed marriage and was searching for a job to support his new family.

Eight months pregnant with Tyler, they were married without fanfare at the Massillon courthouse. Dawn and I blew up balloons and made "Just Married" signs for their car. We ran late and passed them on Lincoln Way as they drove to the Red Roof Inn for their honeymoon. Sue waved at us from the passenger side window.

Chris' parents weren't pleased with all of his choices but allowed him and his new bride to move into their remodeled basement. It helped that Sue did most of the chores around the house. My new brother-in-law worked long hours at a factory, giving up his dream to play baseball. It wasn't ideal. They both struggled to make things work.

After Danny's death, Amy was no longer the center of attention. The baby of Kimmensville had the ideal life, filled with fun and laughter. Now she was surrounded by anger and sadness. Used to stability, everything in her life was now uncertain. She was miserable, but we were too busy to notice.

Our lives were blown apart, and Sue and I were mad as hell. Devastated that we lost our only brother. We wanted someone to blame. Mom wept and walked around in a daze repeating his name and asking why. None of us realized that our behavior made it even harder for our little sister to cope.

One afternoon, Amy disappeared from the trailer. We ran frantically through the neighborhood, searching and yelling her name. I had a sickening feeling in my stomach. Horrible thoughts ran through my mind. Mom was hysterical. She ran around the neighborhood crying *"Amy!!"* like a wounded animal. She could not lose another child. Sue and I never slowed down our search.

We finally found Amy at the bottom of a big box of blankets in the laundry room, still unpacked from our move. She lifted her head and said she was sleeping and didn't hear us. We were so excited to find her safe at home. We all embraced and cried happy tears.

Decades later, Amy admitted that she had hidden from us that afternoon, hearing every scream and cry. Her world had been turned upside down, and we barely noticed her anymore. She was six years old, she wanted attention. Our baby sister was hurting tremendously. She missed Danny and wanted her old life back, everything to be the same. Unfortunately, that would never happen. Amy's life got worse before it improved.

Mom continued to plan our move to Florida. I tried to convince her to allow me to live in California. I would finish my senior year in Carlsbad with Judi and Jim. I enjoyed it so much more than the retirement community in Florida. St. Petersburg, home of the newlywed and the nearly dead.

Aunt Judi and Uncle Jim were up for it. Mom was hesitant. I think she may have gone along with my idea, it didn't matter. Before the school year ended, Uncle Jim's company decided to relocate his position. To Florida. They would be living one hour north of St. Pete. My fate was sealed. I was moving south.

My best friends had thrown a going away bash for me at Dawn's house. Ruthie was happy to host. All night long, the bonfire in the backyard raged, and the music streamed from the stereo. We roasted marshmallows, reminisced, and hugged. They had no idea how much I would miss them. They at least still had each other. We promised to keep in touch.

Sue never hesitated over her decision to stay with Chris. She just wished we had not moved. The day we left, my big sister felt as if her entire family had abandoned her. The tough girl she had now become dried her eyes and once again, buried her sorrow.

Weeks before our move, Mom, Amy, and I packed up our belongings and shipped several boxes to Florida. Always there for us, Grandma stored our things and flew to Ohio to escort Amy while Mom and I made the sixteen-hour drive in her car. We transported fragile items in the backseat, like plants, dishes, and Amy's bird.

That morning, Dawn stopped by to say goodbye and to tape a *"Wally World or Bust"* sign to our back window. We pulled out of our driveway with a luggage carrier strapped to the top and Budgie wedged between boxes and Mom's foliage. We were a sight--all we needed was an old lady tied to the roof.

Mom and I left the poster up the entire trip. It made us smile when people pointed and laughed. We needed the chuckle because we mostly cried.

Mom drove us to Tennessee and rented a hotel room for the night. I snuck the bird into our room, and we crashed on our separate beds. I quietly sobbed myself to sleep, wondering what my life would be like in Florida. We had no idea that our journey had just begun.

Wally World or Bust

The day after we had left Massillon, Grandma and Amy welcomed us to Florida with open arms and baked spaghetti. Mom and I were physically and emotionally exhausted. Both of us picked at our dinner, then collapsed on the pull-out couch for the night.

Luckily for us, Aunt Nancy and Uncle Bob owned an apartment building down the street from Grandma's condo. A two-bedroom apartment was available on the second floor of the Tara House. We moved in that week.

With only babysitting and nursing aide experience on her application, Mom was happy to find work at Kmart as a cashier in the cafeteria. We bought our furniture at the Salvation Army, doing our best to make the apartment comfortable with what we could afford. I registered for my last year of school at Northeast High and hung out at the beach in the afternoons, waiting for my dreaded first day.

Two weeks after we arrived in Florida, I walked into a school with four times the population of Tuslaw. I didn't know a single soul.

Mom enrolled Amy in second grade at the local public elementary, she didn't know anyone either. She was still crying when she walked in the apartment door. I hugged her and asked my little sister what had happened. Through her blubbering, she cried out, "No one knew my *NAME!*"

The next day, unsure of how she could afford it, Mom had transferred my little sister to the Catholic school affiliated with Grandma's church. We knew Amy needed more comfort in her life, not less. Mom would figure it out, she always did.

When Amy walked in the door, the teachers at Holy Name made sure my little sister felt welcome. She never returned to the school that didn't know her name. Grandma not only helped pay the tuition, but she also picked up Amy every day and treated her to a donut or cookie at Kash N' Karry on the way home.

Mom and I were beginning to adjust, but it was hard sharing one car. It was time for my own transportation. Our generous and savvy grandma agreed to lend me money, with a fair interest rate. And, my neighbors, two brothers with connections offered to take me to a car auction.

My winning bid was five hundred dollars for a white 1977 Toyota Corolla. Other than it being eight years old and a stick shift, it was perfect. Because I was unfamiliar with a manual transmission, one of the guys drove it back to our apartment complex.

I was anxious, Mom insisted that I wait until the next afternoon, she would teach me to drive a stick. She promised to be home by four o'clock. I was bored by noon. How hard could it be? I took my new wheels for a spin, gears grinding and screeching the entire way. A few blocks later, I gave up, parked it on the side of the road, and walked home.

After finally learning to drive my car, I added a bumper sticker on the back window. *Don't Drink and Drive You Might Hit a Bump and Spill Your Drink*, seemed to be a perfect choice. The usual reaction was a chuckle, even from a couple of cops idling behind me at a red light. I was happy they liked it because I had a cold beer between my thighs and a joint in my purse. The little Corolla was my dependable ride for four years until I sold it for seven hundred dollars, the decal still intact.

Several weeks after we had arrived in the south, Hurricane Helena hit land on Labor Day weekend. The police

193

careened through the neighborhoods with bullhorns demanding that we all evacuate. The storm was hitting St. Petersburg.

Amy shook me awake at two o'clock, clutching her Cabbage Patch Kid in one arm, her boom box in the other. *"Wake up, Lisa! We have to go!! There's a hurricane coming! Come on, we have to leave now!!"* she cried.

I stumbled to the door, grabbed my purse and jacket, and slipped my feet into a pair of flip flops. Our neighbors on the second floor were milling around the breezeway watching the storm. The seasoned Floridians strongly advised against evacuating, unless you absolutely had to.

Deserting our apartment meant sleeping on the floor of a school gymnasium, where we would be wedged between other sweaty, misplaced bodies, until further notice. If you dared shower, it would be in the locker rooms. Mom shut off our lights and hoped the water would not reach the second floor.

That night we barely slept but knew it was better than the alternative. We woke up to a power outage and a flooded parking lot.

Mom and I lit candles and transferred food from our refrigerator to a cooler. Amy tossed any remaining ice cubes on top. Neighbors began knocking on our door. First, Mom's friend looking for shelter. Then the brothers, holding skim boards and wearing swim trunks and big smiles.

Without hesitation, Amy and I joined them. Sloshing through the parking lot, I passed my car. Water had reached the door handle, but I tried not to panic and optimistically hoped it would start. The salt water would just add to the rustic beauty. When we got bored with skimming, we found an abandoned grocery cart and took turns pushing each other through the puddles.

We survived our first hurricane, but Mom was homesick. She made plans to see Sue and her family for Thanksgiving.

Tyler was two months old, and she was already missing so much. There wasn't enough money for three plane tickets, so Mom and Amy flew to Ohio for a week, and I stayed back.

I had my first Thanksgiving alone, a Lean Cuisine frozen dinner in front of the television. The only thing I cooked up were plans to throw another party.

Since Mom was away, my new friend Laura argued, "We should invite a few people over during the break. Your mom will *never* find out!" I desperately wanted to make friends and impress the few I had, so I went along with it.

Unbeknownst to me, my new buddy advertised the affair to our massive high school. Laura printed the details on sticky notes and smacked them on random lockers throughout Northeast High School.

Before anyone showed up, I had cleared the table tops and hid anything that Mom cared about. When kids I had never seen streamed into our tiny apartment, I knew I'd made one right decision.

A group of guys from the south end of town paraded in, carrying a boom box and a five-gallon water jug fashioned into a bong. Loud rap music screamed from the speakers and smoke trailed them like dirt following Pig Pen.

As the party escalated I lost all control, my pleas to keep it down fell on deaf ears. The front yard and stairwell were packed with teenagers--drinking, smoking, dancing, everyone having a great time, except me.

I was at a loss for what to do. The beers I kept nervously guzzling only hindered my decision-making ability. I finally went to my bedroom, slid my dresser in front of the door as a barricade, and passed out.

I awoke to a booming voice yelling, "*Get out! Everyone out!!*" Uncle Bob stormed through my bedroom door, pushing

195

my dresser aside as if it were a sock, and told me to get up and deal with the mess. Aunt Judi had called to warn me they were coming, I didn't get the message.

By the time I staggered into the living room, most of the kids were gone. They left an absolute mess. Apparently, while I was unconscious, the apartment building manager threatened to call the police. In response, a drunken basketball player punched our landlord in the face and broke his glasses. That's when my aunt and uncle were summoned.

Not my most stellar evening. I was zero for three when it came to hosting parties and could care less about my future.

At school, I skipped every second period to go to McDonald's with my friend Diana. We had the munchies and ordered Egg McMuffins and milkshakes. She was my partner in crime until we had a falling out after being busted at Gandy Beach for curfew violation, as well as a few other infractions.

My friendships and grades reflected what I had put into them. Other than history class, I didn't make much of an effort at school. History was always my weakest subject, but my teacher, Mr. Brown, was hilarious and cute.

During lectures, when he saw droopy eyes and bobbing heads, he recalled a wild story from his college days to amuse us. He also made the content interesting, so I actually studied for his tests, but still only earned a C.

Prior years, I teetered between a 3.8 and 3.9 GPA. At Northeast, I struggled. I was completely disengaged with school, life, and everything in general.

When Amy wasn't around, I opened the window, turned on a fan, and smoked pot in our bedroom. I was also drinking several days a week, staying out late, and making few wise choices.

Diana and I hung out with a couple of guys that turned out to be Venezuelan cocaine dealers. Mom knew them as Manuel and Otto. She never mentioned my poor behavior or declining grades. Mom and I staggered through life while Grandma mostly raised Amy.

Thankfully, a counselor at school noticed my previous GPA and extracurricular activities from Ohio. She suggested I join the Future Business Leaders of America (FBLA) club.

After being accepted, Mrs. Fischer welcomed me to the class. She was thrilled about my shorthand and computer experience. The year I spent at R.G. Drage Technical School paid off. To help me meet other students, she nominated me as the Treasurer of FBLA. She had no idea how much these small gestures meant to me.

A provision of joining the club was a part-time job. Mrs. Fischer handed me an ad for an opening at the *St. Petersburg Times* newspaper. My interview was scheduled for the next afternoon.

I wrapped my long curls in a bun, put on a dress, hose, and high heels before I drove downtown. After the meeting, I was offered and accepted the job as a part-time receptionist in the Purchasing Department.

I wore office attire to school, attended a few classes, and ate lunch on my drive to work. By one o'clock, I was seated behind my wooden desk.

I started my first office position in 1985, before cell phones and computers. All appointments were scheduled by me, either in person or over a landline. Hopeful salespeople dropped by unannounced to see a purchasing agent or leave samples of whatever they were pushing. No one entered without first getting past my desk.

Every semester, Mrs. Fischer, pregnant with her son, made the trek to my office to meet with my manager. Kari gave her positive feedback on my progress and raved about my typing and shorthand skills.

My manager dictated letters to me that I transcribed and typed on company letterhead. My work was the only part of my life where I was actually exceeding anyone's expectations.

The annual FBLA shorthand competition was approaching, and my teacher encouraged me to compete. After a late night out with friends, I almost blew it off. But, not wanting to disappoint Mrs. Fischer, I made the trip to Clearwater.

That Saturday morning, I wandered through the halls of the gigantic high school. Eventually, I found the room marked "Shorthand I." The other stenography aficionados were already sitting in front of typewriters.

Moments before the timer began ticking away, I slid into an empty chair and dug in my purse for a pen. A teacher paced across the front of the room, dictating a business letter. We all madly scribbled in our notebooks.

After jotting down the closing remarks, we spun our chairs towards the typewriters and translated our own scrawl. The next week, I was shocked to learn that I had won first place. I was headed to Orlando for the next round of competition.

Mrs. Fischer chaperoned the trip, driving all five of us kids that won a business competition. I didn't place in the Regionals, but more importantly, I made friends and had a blast.

We ran around the hotel floors, swam in the pool, soaked in the hot tub, and danced the conga line at the banquet dinner. Things were starting to turn around, and I realized that I did have a future if I wanted one.

Mom was coming to the same realization about her life. Post-divorce, Mom's best friend followed her to Florida. Sorry to see Barb's marriage end, Mom was thrilled she chose St. Pete as her new residency and helped her get a job. They not only supported one another, but they also worked alongside each other for years at the Health and Human Services office.

The besties hung out on weekends, enjoyed the beaches, the sunshine, and everything Florida had to offer. They were both young, beautiful women and eventually started dating single men.

Always in sync, Mom and Barb both made a big mistake and remarried a couple of losers. After our mom had married Deadbeat Dave in the courthouse, she carried a bouquet of grocery store flowers into our apartment and shared the disturbing news. Amy and I sobbed.

Within weeks of their wedding, her new husband had lost his job and spent his days sleeping on our couch. When he was awake, he mooched off of Mom and dreamed up meals he could make with onions. Onions were Amy's archenemy, refusing to eat even a sliver of the pungent vegetable.

Mom worked the evening shift at Kmart, so Dave cooked us dinner. Every night, Amy looked at her plate and saw the translucent chunks sticking out of her meal. She bowed her head and cried. My dinner conversation with my new stepfather started every night with, "She doesn't *like onions, Dave!*" While I defended her, the sadistic bum demanded that she eat every bite.

Oh, how I despised the way he treated us, especially my helpless sister. One night, I threatened to move out. Dave agreed, "Go for it, *slut!*"

So I did.

I had just barely graduated from Northeast with a 2.8 GPA. My high school career did not end well. I received my first failing grade in the second period, freshman science. And, I intentionally botched my SAT.

I spent about fifteen minutes coloring in the bubbles on the Scantron sheet. I was satisfied with my rendition of a Christmas tree adorned with lights and ornaments. The first to walk out the door, I tossed the card into the box labeled *Completed SAT Tests*. It was Saturday, which meant my friends were waiting for me at Harry's Beach Bar.

Mrs. Fischer saved me from total disgrace. She chose me as the recipient of the Future Business Leader of America Award for the class of 1986. During the awards ceremony, I was shocked to hear my name called out for anything. I walked on the stage to accept the honor, and then humbly returned to my seat in the auditorium. It was a thrilling feeling to know someone believed that I could be successful, even when I didn't.

At eighteen-years-old, I moved in with my pothead boyfriend and never moved back home. I met Mom and Amy for breakfast on Sundays, attended my little sister's baseball games, and never missed Grandma's baked spaghetti dinners.

Shortly after I left, Mom and Barb both realized the error of their ways and divorced the scumbags they so poorly chose to marry. The day Mom kicked Dave out, he stopped by the ATM machine and emptied her savings account. She was broke but happy.

I was so proud of my mom for her courage, and Amy was thrilled. Later, I asked her, "Why did you *marry him*?" She answered, "Because he brought me flowers and paid me compliments." Mom never had a lot of self-esteem, but I didn't realize how incredibly sad and lonely she had been.

As hard as Mom tried to support herself and Amy, their financial situation continued to decline. Thanks to Dave, the small amount of money she had left from the divorce was gone. Dad was now only sending a child support check for one kid, and she was working minimum wage jobs.

I wasn't much help, spending my time with crazy, fun-loving kids who liked to party. I was three years away from the legal drinking age, still using Sue's ID to get into clubs. I tried any drug put in front of me, I was shoplifting, drinking and driving, and lying to my family. I was comfortably numb.

After Dave and I had moved out, Mom and Amy moved to a smaller apartment, but couldn't afford it for long. They ended up in government housing. Amy and the neighbor kids played on a swing set that was always surrounded by puddles of mud. Mosquitoes swarming and stinging. My dear sister not only came home with bug bites but also had perpetual lice that they could not rid.

Mom also qualified for other government subsidies. She took full advantage of them to support her daughter. When Mom told me she waited in line for blocks of cheese and bought their groceries with food stamps, I cried. They never complained, but after every visit, I left distraught and helpless.

I was not doing any better, living with my drug-obsessed boyfriend and throwing parties on the weekends. I went completely off the rails for a few years, forgetting the promise I made to Danny. I was definitely not living the life he would have wanted for me, or himself.

I made the first move, which was not a pretty scene, and ditched Tony. Doreen, my only stable friend, was there for me when I needed her the most. She had seen me struggle and make bad choices for years, but she still stayed close by. Her brother-in-law helped me pick up my broken furniture from the front yard and move anything salvageable to storage.

Her sister had just moved out. Malyn's room was free, and their parents were kind enough to let me stay there for a while. For the first time, I had *my own bedroom*. Her mom knew I needed security and took me under her wing as if I was her own daughter. I was lucky enough to two more strong women enter my life.

201

My new boyfriend was interviewing for jobs on the west coast. Dean had recently separated, and his two kids were being raised by their mother in Alberta, Canada. He missed them terribly and wanted to be closer to his children. When he was offered an executive position with the *San Francisco Chronicle*, he asked me to join him. I was finally moving to California!

About the same time, Mom was contemplating a move back to Ohio. She tried her best to make it in Florida but wanted to help raise her grandchildren. Sue and Chris just had their second son, Ryan, Mom was ready to go back home. Or so she thought.

When we announced our departures to Grandma, she was happy for us, but would also miss us terribly, especially Amy. Our family was being split even further apart, living on opposite coasts now.

On Dean's birthday, June 13, 1990, Mom and Amy drove us to the airport. I was excited about our adventure but inconsolable that I had to leave my remaining family. Once again, I cried the entire trip.

There was one piece of advice I didn't take from Doreen's mom. She warned me not to move to California with my boyfriend, "until he put a ring on my finger." I hugged her and assured her that I wanted to take that risk. If it didn't work out, I could come back to Florida or find my way in California--I was a survivor. I also had learned an essential lesson from my parents. It takes more than a ring to feel safe and secure in a relationship.

Mom's Acting Funny

A year after Dean and I had settled into our apartment in San Francisco, I received a strange call from Sue. She started the conversation by saying, "Mom's acting funny, Lisa." Confused, I asked for examples. My big sister recanted several concerns, none of them humorous.

I immediately flew to Ohio and saw for myself. Our mother, the social butterfly, wouldn't leave the house. When I walked in the door, she was sitting at the kitchen table in her robe. She turned her head towards me, I saw dark, empty eyes looking back.

Mom had just been fired from her cashiering job at a grocery store. A police officer came through her line, and she called him a devil before running and screaming through the parking lot. At home, she stopped paying her bills, showering, and getting dressed. Mom now spent her days shuffling around in her pajamas and staring out of windows.

We told ourselves she just needed a vacation. Massillon revived a flood of memories that she had suppressed living in Florida. The ghosts she ran from she now had to face.

She was not capable of flying alone, so we called dependable Aunt Judi. She and my cousin Tommy graciously agreed to pick up my mom and drive her to Judi's home on Hernando Beach.

Jim and Judi's haven, nicknamed Verzulliland, was a relaxing paradise. My uncle Jim Verzulli designed their stilt house on the Gulf of Mexico so they could witness every sunrise and sunset. Over the years, they added a hot tub, boat, jet ski, kayak, tiki bar, and cabana for overnight visitors. Their guests never want to leave.

Even in that idyllic setting, the report we received from Judi about Mom's state of mind was worrisome. One morning, she became agitated and paranoid. My cousin Tommy had just stopped by Verzulliland to visit. A huge grin spread across Mom's face, she jumped up and hugged him tightly. When she pulled away, she looked at him and said, *"Danny!"* Mom hugged him again, then buried her face in his chest. Tommy froze, looking to his family for guidance. They were stunned and sad but knew they had to call for help.

This episode happened in 1991, seven years after my brother's death. It was Mom's first breakdown, and wouldn't be her last. She spent three days in the Florida hospital, then rested at her older sister's house. Nancy also lived on the water, we hoped another few days of rest would be all she needed.

The following weekend, one of her brothers drove her home to Ohio so she could receive care from her physician. And because my sisters wanted her nearby.

Sue and Chris immediately admitted Mom to the local hospital for evaluation. My sister insisted, and the nurse promised to keep her for the night. When Sue called to check on her progress the next morning, she was curtly informed that our mother had been transferred. Based on their assessment, she was a candidate for the Massillon Psychiatric Center! Mom was suddenly a patient of the formerly named Hospital for the Insane. We knew the real, unspoken reason for the eviction was her lack of medical insurance.

I made another trip to Ohio and set up appointments with her doctors. Sue and I begged them to transfer her elsewhere. The administrators refused our pleas and kept our mother for four grueling months.

There was nothing we could do but watch this beautiful soul deteriorate in front of us. Sue and I visited her a few times alone before we dressed Amy up and snuck her in to see Mom.

Minors were not allowed entry into the facility, but a pair of heels, makeup, and skirt fooled the guard.

It was terrifying to see our mom in such a depressed state. She was withering away both physically and mentally, eventually refusing to eat or talk. Some of the other patients screamed all day.

An angry young man spent hours marching up and down the hallway, his fists balled as he yelled profanities at no one. Other residents shouted back from their rooms, "*Shut Up!!*" I wanted to be tough for my mom, but I could never get through a visit without weeping.

Amy had moved in with Sue, and I fought with the Disability and Social Security offices. Sue and Chris were renting a two-bedroom townhouse, Tyler and Ryan already shared the second bedroom. They didn't have much room for a fourteen-year-old girl, but they were more than happy to squeeze her in.

Our big sister made up a comfortable area in their basement with a bed and dresser. Lacking a closet, Amy hung her clothes from the water pipes that ran along the ceiling. She was sad but grateful to have Sue and Chris in her life.

Mom was finally released from the inhumane place that provided more medication than therapy. The psychiatric hospital sent her home with an armful of prescriptions for severe depression and a lifetime reminder of her stay--Hepatitis B.

In spite of the faulty, mental health system, two years later, she was once again, a functioning adult. Mom was doing well enough to work part-time and rent her own place. My little sister was so excited to have her own bedroom again, Mom gave her the largest room. Amy joined the cheerleading squad at school and, for once, appeared to have the life of an average teenager.

Mom continued to improve until a quack at a government-subsidized medical facility advised her to stop taking her prescriptions. Several weeks later, the similar symptoms returned, and Sue and Amy became suspicious. When they quizzed Mom, she admitted that she had stopped taking her meds.

I received another late-night call from my Sue. "Mom's acting funny," was now our code. I told her I would be right there.

Amy's turbulent world was about to spiral out of control again. The fall of 1994, I walked through the door of the creaky, old house they rented on Wooster Street. Mom was rocking back and forth in her recliner watching a television sitcom. Sue and Chris were silently huddled on the sofa with their boys, Amy sat next to them, their eyes as round as saucers.

Mom turned her head, and without getting up said, "Hi, Lisa." Then she turned back towards the television. When I came home, I'd been used to hugs and kisses. Things had definitely declined again.

Mom shook her head at the television comedy and said, "I wish they would turn off this *porn*." Sue hit the power button on the remote, and we all sat in silence as Mom rocked back and forth.

That night, I collapsed on an air mattress in Amy's room and planned my next day, tears streaming down my face. It was my turn to admit our mother. First, I would make an appointment with her psychiatrist, just to be sure.

Amy left early for school, but I wasn't ready to face the day. I tossed and turned, finally falling back asleep. Unsure of how much time had passed, I opened my eyes to my mom standing over my bed. She was wringing her hands, an eerie smile on her face. I jumped up and asked her if everything was alright. She smiled but didn't answer me.

I grabbed my clothes, ran into the bathroom and told her I would be right back. As I splashed my face with water and brushed my teeth, I revised the plan. There was no time for an appointment. We would leave immediately and sit in the doctor's office waiting room until he had an opening. Shaking, I shimmied into my jeans, threw on a T-shirt, and opened the door.

I rushed into Amy's room. Mom was gone. On my way to the kitchen, I noticed the basement door was open. I poked my head in the opening and saw her descending the stairs. "Mom! Where are you going? I was going to make us coffee," trying my best not to scare her. She turned around, looked up at me, and sadly answered, "I thought I would just get it over with and hang myself."

I ran down the stairs, put my arm around her shoulders. We carefully walked to Mom's bedroom. Tears dripped down my face as I helped her change into her clothes.

We drove to the doctor's office where he took us right away. After a short exam, we were referred to the hospital. A nurse was waiting and took us to her assigned bed in the psychiatric ward.

I met her new physician who explained as much as she could about what was happening before discussing treatment options. Mom had suffered such tremendous loss and heartache in her life that she willed herself to shut down. She couldn't take any more. I understood. Life is often too hard for sensitive people, Mom just wasn't able to cope with her son's suicide.

After one of the longest days of my life, I hugged my sweet mother and told her how much I loved her. Barely able to hold myself together, I drove back to Sue's house.

My manager at work was incredibly understanding. Nonetheless, I could only stay a few more days. I felt terrible always leaving Sue to deal with the aftermath. She was such a giving person and said she didn't mind. She had a full-time job and family, I know it was difficult for them. Every time I left, I felt so guilty.

Mom's stay at the hospital lasted much longer this time. She lost more weight and refused to talk. The pharmaceutical cocktails they prescribed had no effect. We knew this episode was severe when her doctor suggested Electroconvulsive Therapy (ECT) treatments.

Once again, my big sister carried the burden. And I absolutely supported her decisions every step of the way. Required to watch videotapes of an ECT procedure, Sue now knew what Mom was about to endure.

She called me afterward, her voice trembling. Sue described the video and compared it to being electrocuted. The doctor insisted it was the only option left. We hesitantly agreed, knowing we had exhausted all other alternatives. Sue, Amy, and I just wanted our mother back.

Eight different times they strapped Mom to a gurney. The nurse placed a plastic band with wires on her head and hooked her up to a machine. Then, a rubber mouth guard was inserted to prevent her from biting her tongue.

The doctor flipped a switch, the machine came to life. The electric currents passed through Mom's brain, triggering intentional seizures. We felt like monsters before every treatment. Sue and I had assured each other the procedure was supposed to revive the lost functionality in her mind.

Thankfully, it worked.

Soon after, Mom was released into Sue's care with even more medication. One bottle treated anti-psychosis, another severe depression. The third pill was a sleeping aid, and the fourth claimed to relieve the symptoms brought on by the other three.

While Sue tended to Mom and Amy, along with her own family, I continued my battle with the Ohio Disability office. Amy was a junior in high school when I finally won. Mom was approved for temporary benefits. At last, a hard-won victory that provided all of us a bit of a respite.

Her struggle with the loss of her son continues today. How could it not? Mom still keeps Danny's robe hanging in her closet. She kisses it every morning when she wakes up and every night before she goes to sleep.

His memorabilia is safely stored in Mom's closet. Including his pencil sketches that we found several months after his passing. When we moved his dresser, we heard something slide down the wall behind it. A cardboard box stuffed with Danny's drawings was lying on the floor. I flipped through the stack, quickly searching for the sad, little boy he was drawing the last time I saw him alive. It wasn't there.

We all survived Danny's suicide in our own way. I learned to love, laugh, hope, and dream in Kimmensville, with no worries in the world. When things did take the worst possible turn we could have ever imagined, we prevailed.

I learned forgiveness from my mother. My brother taught me to never take a moment for granted. And today my sisters keep me laughing. We never hang up a call without saying, "I love you!" I promised Amy because she was so young when we lost our brother, that I would always share my Danny Stories. In that spirit, I was led down the path to the memories you see here.

Epilogue

Kimmensville was a place in time, the dream of five families. Our population briefly topped out at twenty-five, but the carefree community could not sustain. The welcoming signs came down. The pothole-ridden road is now paved and lined with single-family homes.

Sandy's mom and Karlene's dad still bookend the neighborhood today. Their spouses sadly passed away, including our Mayor Ronnie. Everyone else has moved on.

Everything changed the night Dad's truck sped down the driveway in New Philadelphia as Mom yelled out the open window, *"Amy! Danny had an accident!! We're going to the hospital!!"* Mom and Dad didn't return to pick her up. Instead, she saw her brother one last time, in a casket.

Amy didn't understand what was going on, why Danny was gone. She was angry and hurt, her perfect world disrupted, her carefree life as the baby of Kimmensville was over. She was terrified. The once safe environment was replaced with so many insecurities. Financial burdens, moving from apartment to apartment, an overwhelming sadness—this would become her new world. Amy struggled more than any of us knew. She didn't want to bring more grief to her already distraught family, so she hid her pain.

In spite of the mayhem that was her childhood, or maybe because of it, my little sister excelled in everything she set out to do. She was the first person in our immediate family to earn a college degree, funded primarily through scholarships and grants. She married her handsome college sweetheart, and not surprisingly, became a Registered Nurse.

Amy longed for a life of stability and structure and built a beautiful, loving home surrounded by her strong Christian beliefs. But a few years later, Amy's life was once again uprooted, her strength tested.

Hours after a premature birth that neither the doctors nor Amy could control, she and her husband lost their twin babies. That day, the fear and uncertainty that still rules within her returned. My little sister and Jason helplessly held their beautiful infants, Kaden and Kaci, until they were no more.

When she called me with the terrible news, the heartbreak in her voice was gut wrenching. I wanted to fix her pain so badly. After we had hung up, I screamed to whoever was listening, *"Enough already!!"*

My determined little sister went to all lengths to bring her next set of twins, Landen and Braxton, into this world. The year they turned six, she and Jason celebrated the birth of their youngest son, Carson, who happens to be the spitting image of our brother, Danny.

They are providing the secure childhood for their boys that she lost at such an early age. Including the positive influence of Mother Goose, now Grandma Goose to the kids and babysitter for the next generation. I'm so proud of my little sister, she is doing an incredible job at life.

If there was a positive outcome for our dad, he built a special bond with Amy. After we had moved to Florida, he often flew her to Ohio to visit. Dad became Amy's rock and her primary financial support system during college.

To this day, he is always there for her and her family. Dad kept true to his word when he told Sue and me that day in the hospital that he wanted to be a better father. Dad had another chance with Amy, and he seized it.

My parents get along better now than they did during their marriage. The whole family spends every holiday and special occasion together, Dad and his wife often hosting.

During this journey, I did quite a bit of reflection about my dad. I actually feel incredibly sad for him. He has to live with what happened as much as we all do, but he knows Danny was angry with him.

He was a young father doing his best to support his family and instill some order. Every parent makes mistakes, but Dad does not deserve to carry the burden he must have in his heart. I'm glad he has Carol and his beagle, Scooter.

Mom is still a happy person and considers everyone she meets a friend. After everything she's been through, she is one of the most optimistic people you'll ever meet and honestly lives life to the fullest. It's astonishing that her positive outlook was not affected by the misfortunes in her life. Mom is a fantastic role model. Danny would be pleased about that.

Sadly, she will always struggle with depression and be at the mercy of the mental health system. A system that disgraces our country. The summer of Danny's thirtieth anniversary, another medical clod changed her prescription.

The familiar and scary signs returned. Mom spent a few weeks in the hospital ridding her system of the erroneous medication she was taking. The doctors found a pharmaceutical cocktail that worked, and Mom was back!

Sue continued to be a caretaker and raised three beautiful boys. While her friends in high school were planning their futures, deciding which college to attend or career to start, all she wanted was to be a mother. Giving Becky up left such a void in her life. When Sue found out she was pregnant with Tyler, she had been secretly thrilled.

Sue regularly visits Tyler and his daughter in New York and just as often heads south to see Becky, Eric, and her two grandchildren in Florida. They've been calling her Granny since she was forty-five-years-old, and she loves it.

Her best friend and soul mate, Kevin, shares her belief that you always put family first. He walked into this messy clan with a warm and loving heart and never looked back. They have been stable support systems for each other, Sue always being there for Kevin during his family tragedies, as well.

It's not easy for my big sister to forgive and forget, she experienced too much hurt. After witnessing so much agony, she's realistic about life and our inevitable end. The pain and loss Sue has endured rivals Mom and Amy's. She soldiers on with her quick and sarcastic sense of humor.

My big sis spends her days providing joy and happiness to elderly people who don't have many days left on this earth and gives them a reason to laugh and smile. Sue is the strongest woman I have ever met, and I am so proud to call her my sister.

When my life changed, I suppressed so many feelings. At first, I rebelled. Then, I smiled and moved on, as if everything was fine. Clearly, things weren't okay when I almost crashed and burned in Florida. Dean was my knight in shining armor, swooping in at a crucial point in my life and whisking me away to California.

Arriving on the west coast with our personal belongings, mismatched dishes, and a cracked microwave, we were literally starting over. Dean was also mending a broken heart, living so far away from his two children was crushing him. Moving to California made his visits to Calgary much easier.

We supported each other as we both struggled with our losses, and were thrilled to start our lives together in a place that didn't carry the daily reminders of what we missed.

I had the promise to keep to my little brother. I finally got my act together and became unwavering about not wasting my life. I attended night school to pursue a business degree while I worked full-time.

I used my office skills from high school and experience from the *St. Petersburg Times* to start my career at a Fortune 500 financial institution in downtown San Francisco.

After being inspired by a college Humanities class, I became an active volunteer in the community and still work closely with the urban youth. Dean and I relished everything San Francisco Bay Area had to offer, and we traveled around the country on his business trips, always anxious to return.

I know Danny hadn't intended to devastate the girls he loved the most, but it ripped our hearts out and threw our lives into a tailspin. Over the past three decades, his death caused us all a tremendous amount of pain and suffering. It always will.

It was a hell of a long and bumpy road. If I didn't have the mentors, family, and friends in my life to guide me through this storm, I honestly am not sure where I would be today.

This process has been an incredibly therapeutic experience for my sisters and me. We cried a river of tears remembering the details. While it was hard to relive the sad parts, it was healing to finally talk about how it truly affected us.

I had many second thoughts about writing this book because of my father. My intention was never to hurt anyone. Actually, the opposite. My stories are the facts--as my sisters, Aunt Judi, Mom, my best friends, and I recall them. I also included Danny's drawings so I can share his incredible talent that never reached its full potential.

My family reminisces over some of these anecdotes at family gatherings. We laugh at our mischief and cry about our losses. My goal was to thoughtfully tell the story about our unique childhood and my gentle and selfless brother, from a sibling's perspective.

If you recognize a loved one suffering, or if you relate to Danny, please know there is help. Know that *someone* cares. We are *never* alone, and we *always* have options. As my good friend Mark David said to me, "Believe there's a light at the end of the tunnel. Believe you might be that light for someone else."

Acknowledgements

Thank you to the residents of Kimmensville, my family, and my comrades--Sandra Lowers, Karlene Rittmaier, Jimmy Espinosa, Tommy, Andy and Colleen Black, Sue King, and Amy Kubbins. The parents of Kimmensville allowed us to have the most carefree, spontaneous, creative, and loving childhood. I hope you enjoy this keepsake of our memories, the good and the bad. I love you all.

Thank you to all of my beautiful friends that were my cheerleaders during this process. And to those of you that read my drafts and gave me honest feedback and encouragement to continue. Dean, Miranda, Sue, Amy, Mom, Aunt Judi, Aunt Nancy, Colleen, Dawn Harper, Tami Schmutzler, Donna Jeffers, Nancy Hoffman, Hank Donat (also for the cover idea), John Yatsko, Roger Schefers, Lauren Kennedy, Charlie Shields, Jeff Raymond, Lori Goracke, Maria Rada, Linda Calderone, Patty Urda, Lisa Fierro, Mary Church, Ilse Miranda, and my MNO gals.

A serendipitous meeting on the #4 Golden Gate bus led me to my editor, Thomas Centolella. I cannot thank you enough for your thoughtful advice, feedback, and time, TC. You were invaluable during this process, I could not have finished this without you. You are an inspiring teacher and poet.

My talented and creative daughter worked endless hours on various ideas for a cover, while madly completing college applications and submitting drawing portfolios. Thank you for your patience and the amazing end result, Miranda. I am so excited to see what you do in life with your talent.

Mark David, thank you for your coaching advice over the years, for allowing me to use your quote, and for assigning me a project to do something creative. This is the end result.

RIP

Danny Gossage
Grandma Alice Black
Grandpa Howard Black
Great-aunt Margaret Black
Grandpa Charles Gossage
Grandma Mary Gossage
Uncle Bob Sulte
Uncle John Strohm
Dena Strohm
Ronnie Lowers
Bev Kulik
Kaden and Kaci Kubbins
Kathleen Black
Kathy Kuruc
Colleen Wagley

Danny's Drawings

2/84

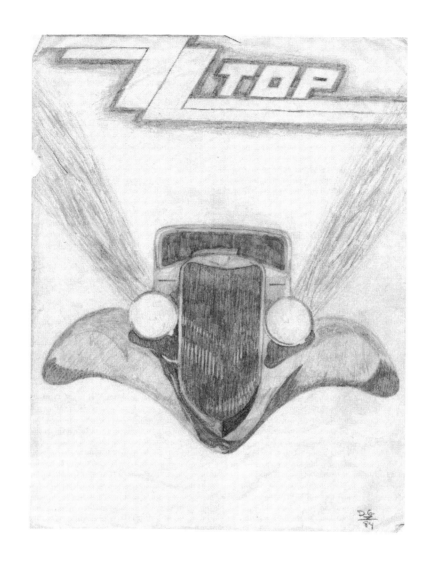

D6
——
84

2/84

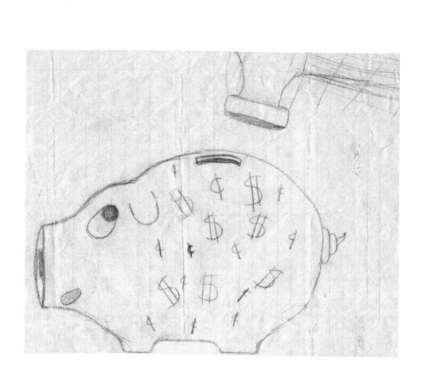

STANLEY STRAWBERRY   BENNY BANANA

PATTY PEACH   OSCAR ORANGE

SHERRY CHERRY   ANGELA APPLE

GARY GRAPE   PAMELA PEAR

PATRICK PINEAPPLE   CONNIE COCONUT

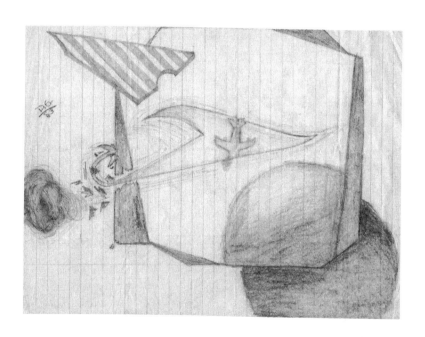

FATHER
TIME

Made in the USA
Lexington, KY
31 July 2017